DIRTY THIRTIES DESPERADOES

Forgotten Victims of the Great Depression

RICH MOLE

VICTORIA · VANCOUVER · CALGARY

Heritage House Publishing Company Ltd.
heritagehouse.ca

Library and Archives Canada Cataloguing in Publication
Mole, Rich, 1946–
Dirty thirties desperadoes : forgotten victims of the Great Depression / Rich Mole.

(Amazing stories)
Issued also in electronic format.
ISBN 978-1-926613-95-6

1. Criminals—Canada—Biography. 2. Depressions—1929—Canada. 3. Canada—Social conditions—1930–1939. I. Title. II. Series: Amazing stories (Surrey, B.C.)

HV6805.M64 2011   364.15'52092271   C2011-900345-7

Series editor: Lesley Reynolds.
Proofreader: Liesbeth Leatherbarrow.
Cover design: Chyla Cardinal. Interior design: Frances Hunter.
Cover photo: Illustration detail from "The Mounties Win the Battle of Banff," unidentified American pulp magazine, spring 1936. Courtesy Whyte Museum of the Canadian Rockies.

The interior of this book was produced using 100% post-consumer recycled paper, processed chlorine free and printed with vegetable-based inks.

Heritage House acknowledges the financial support for its publishing program from the Government of Canada through the Canada Book Fund (CBF), Canada Council for the Arts and the province of British Columbia through the British Columbia Arts Council and the Book Publishing Tax Credit.

18 17 16 15   2 3 4 5
Printed in Canada

Contents

Prologue

IN THE SOUTHEAST-SASKATCHEWAN *mining town of Estevan, 22 Mounties took up positions across Fourth Street. Moving closer was a cavalcade of more than 400 Communist-led striking miners and their wives and girlfriends, taunting, laughing and waving banners that read, "We Refuse to Starve; Down with the Company Store." It was the afternoon of Tuesday, September 29, 1931. The tidy little town was about to become a battlefield in the RCMP's new war on Reds.*

An order was barked, and the Mounties slid their revolvers from their holsters. Smashed by a demonstrator's piece of wood, the chief of Estevan's tiny three-man police service fell, his head streaming blood. Brandishing a crowbar, striker Nick Nargan jumped onto a parked red-and-chrome pumper truck. Volunteer firemen dropped the hose and ran. "Captured, captured!" Nick screamed, his crowbar lifted defiantly. He brought his bar down, smashing at the pumper. A police service revolver cracked. The crowbar clanged to the pavement, and Nick clutched his chest and toppled over. The strikers went wild. Cringing under a hail of rocks and bricks, the rookie Mounties fired their revolvers, reloaded and fired again. When the shooting stopped, three miners lay dead or dying, and 13 others, including innocent residents, sought help for gunshot wounds.

The deadly incident sent shockwaves nationwide. At RCMP Depot Division in Regina, 125 miles north, 20-year-old Ottawa-born Gray Campbell and other raw recruits would receive new training in army weaponry. Some 75 miles farther north, three bored, impoverished teenagers of Doukhobor heritage heard what others said: Estevan was just the latest example of the brutality their Russian grandparents came to Canada to escape.

1

Changing Times

STANDING CLOSE TO THE BONFIRE made wiry little Joe Posnikoff hot and itchy, but the seven-year-old didn't back away. Something was going to happen, and he didn't want to miss it. The Posnikoffs had made the long journey from their farm near Arran, Saskatchewan, to a village called Veregin, mingling with more people than Joe had ever seen in one place. Wagons and buggies had rolled out from Pelly, Buchanan and nearby Kamsack, too. These people were just like the Posnikoffs—Doukhobors.

Burning of Arms

In the language of Joe's people, "Doukhobor" means "spirit wrestlers." Joe wasn't sure exactly what that meant, but he knew it wasn't good. At school, the English-speaking kids said "Doukhobor" with their noses wrinkled, as if they smelled cow shit on his boots. When he and his parents went to Arran to buy supplies, some grown-up English-speakers looked at them the same way the kids at school did.

It made Joe wonder. Canada had so badly wanted the Doukhobors to start farms that it gave them the land—his father told him—so why did people shun them? Was it because his mother and other Doukhobor women dressed in long handmade skirts behind colourful *zanaveski* (aprons) and wore white *platki* (kerchiefs) that covered their close-cropped hair? Little Joe wasn't sure.

The day before, Joe had asked his father why they were travelling so far. To celebrate the burning of arms, his father answered. Joe's brothers, Fred and Harry, had their big ears hanging out, as usual. That night, when the boys were close to sleep, Fred wondered why people would want to burn their arms. Wouldn't it hurt? Joe chuckled. "Arms" meant guns, he whispered. His answer satisfied Fred and Harry, but it only got Joe wondering again. The only people he had seen carrying guns were those red-uniformed policemen. When the Posnikoffs visited Pelly, Joe had sneaked a look at the brown holster riding high on a policeman's broad belt. What would that gun feel like in his hand? What would it feel like to actually shoot it?

After the Posnikoff's wagon rattled out of the barnyard, another question popped into Joe's head. Why did Spirit

Wrestlers burn their guns? His father glanced back with a funny look. Not just guns, George Posnikoff said, turning back to the team, but swords too. In the days before his grandparents had come to Canada, the Russian leader had been the czar. Doukhobors were soldiers in the czar's army. They burned their arms because they didn't want to fight and kill. Many Doukhobors believed God lived inside every person. Killing someone was like killing God.

Joe considered this. If God lived somewhere inside him, He was sure quiet. Joe never felt Him moving, never heard His voice. Maybe He'd never been there, or maybe He'd left. Maybe God didn't want to live inside Joe, after all.

Maybe this czar had been like Canada's king, Joe decided. Joe's teacher had told them about rulers. No, the king lived in England, he reminded himself. The Canadian ruler was the Prime-something-or-other. The teacher's English words confused Joe and that made him angry. To make himself feel better, Joe silently recited words that other kids didn't know, like *edinolichniki*. That's what the Posnikoffs and other Doukhobor families who owned their own land called themselves.

When Joe's parents had been kids, the *edinolichniki* had left prairie Doukhobor villages like Vosnesinia and Osvobozhdeniye (let the teacher try to say those names!). It was the only way each family could own its own land. Most *edinolichniki* still had their farms, but those old villages—20 of them alone around nearby Pelly and Arran—were almost all gone. Times changed, and the land the villagers had worked so hard to make into productive farms was snatched away by the government and sold off, simply because the villagers refused to swear an oath of allegiance to the king.

Following other wagons, the Posnikoffs turned into a field close to the ornate, two-storey house of Doukhobor leader Peter P. Verigin. They parked their wagon among the dozens of others and walked over to a large fire. What Joe saw reminded him of a Sunday *sobranie*, the weekly "meeting of the people." Around the fire, men formed one ring and the women formed another behind them. Everyone said the *Otchie Nash* (the Lord's Prayer, the teacher called it), the women sang psalms, and then one of the old men spoke about long-ago days in Russia, about Doukhobor soldiers who didn't want to kill anyone.

Branches and logs were heaped onto the bonfire, and the flames leaped higher. Men walked up and threw pieces of wood carved in the shape of guns into the blaze. Joe was disappointed—it was all make-believe! Another man stepped up. Joe knew instinctively he was no Doukhobor, but what caught Joe's eye was what the man was holding: real guns! Silently, the stranger began tossing those guns onto the fire, one after the other. Joe stood transfixed. Flames crept across the wooden stocks and flickered around the metal barrels. Joe wanted to reach out and touch those guns, but there was no way he could do that with everyone watching. Besides, those guns would soon be too hot to touch. One day, maybe . . .

Black Thursday

Perspiring under the hot lights, 17-year-old Gray Campbell was chalking the latest quotes on the wall-mounted blackboards in the customer room of an Ottawa stock brokerage. New York Stock Exchange (NYSE) clerks typed the latest prices and trade volumes into Thomas Edison's telegraphic gizmo, the stock ticker, and minutes later, in brokerage houses all over the US and Canada, little machines squatting on wooden pedestals spat those figures out on ribbons of ticker tape. If an investor wanted to watch his profits growing, he motored down to his broker, walked into the customer's room, sat back, lit up and watched someone like Gray Campbell, ticker tape in hand, chalk the changes.

The investors sitting in their easy chairs behind Gray weren't just rich tycoons anymore. As the market grew hot, banks and brokerages started making investment loans to people who had never stepped inside a boardroom or studied a balance sheet: stenographers, jazz musicians, mechanics, teachers and civil servants. Who cared if 20 percent interest was charged? Working stiffs bought stocks on "margin" (finance jargon that sounded nicer than "loan"), confident they would make thousands of dollars.

"Damn, isn't this just the greatest time to be alive?" the boys asked each other over brown-bag lunches. For young brokerage employees like Gray Campbell, who'd been on the job a mere three weeks, the sky was the limit! But Gray didn't give a darn about getting in on "the inside track" of the market. Every day he went home hot, bored and irritable. Meanwhile, his father complained that Gray didn't give a darn about much of anything. He had finished school and had his future to consider. Gray *was* considering it, but he was as dead set against Kingston's Royal Military College as his father seemed dead set on his enrolment there.

However, on October 24, 1929, work was more interesting than usual. Even before the exchange opened, it was standing room only inside Gray's customer room. The day before had been a shocker. In the final hour of trading, a stunning 2.6 million shares had changed hands, as many as usually traded in an entire day. Worse, prices had dropped. This Thursday morning, investors were nervous. Would the market rally? It always had done so before.

Eight hours' drive south, the sight outside the NYSE rendered even the most blasé New Yorker speechless. Hundreds of thousands of people stood before the six massive Corinthian columns, staring at the entrance doors. It wasn't the doors that captivated the crowd but a scarcely human sound coming from behind them. Inside, a thousand frantic men screamed one word, over and over: sell, sell, sell!

A few minutes after the exchange's opening gong, every customer watching Gray Campbell had lost money. By midafternoon, the ticker tape Gray held was useless. The "latest" figures were hours old, even with the ticker clicking away at the unprecedented speed of 500 characters a minute.

Chain-smoking investors frantically demanded that

their reps sell their holdings, but in order for a broker to do that, he had to get through to the exchange. Forget it; the dozen young men who manned the NYSE telephone switchboards were swamped with frantic calls, and ticker clerks couldn't change quotes fast enough. On the day Gray's Roaring Twenties generation would always call "Black Thursday," floor traders were finding few buyers. Four days later, on horrific "Bloody Monday," Friday's relative calm was shattered as prices continued to fall.

The board boys now noticed something unsettling. Behind closed doors, brokerage reps were making tense client calls. The boys could guess what had been said: "Hello, Mr. Wilson? There's been another break in the market. I think you'd better get down here to cover your margin." "Covering margin" drove desperate investors to empty savings accounts, smash piggy banks and snatch up mattress money trying to come up with cash and avoid the inevitable. Soon, brokerage men stopped making repeated calls to a client. If there was no answer, they sold the poor sap's stock out from under him at a fraction of what he bought it for, likely leaving him still owing the broker.

It didn't take a genius to figure out that Gray's job was on the line. He started looking for other employment, just like the millions who were already jobless. Suddenly, nobody was hiring. Almost in desperation, Gray joined the Canadian Militia; at least he would be with friends. A brokerage client had taken a shine to the worried teenager and told him that one organization was still hiring young men. Gray was smart and would pass the exams without any trouble. He should try the Royal Canadian Mounted Police.

A Backcountry Kindness

Bill Neish yanked at the diamond hitch holding his grub and gear firmly on his pack horse. He was itching to head out into the backcountry. After a quick peck from the wife, he was in the saddle and off down the trail. It would be days before he was back at the cabin. Being married was peachy and all, but out here in the Rockies—well, what could a man say? Being a Banff National Park game warden was a fine life, especially on a crisp, early autumn morning after one of the hottest summers wardens could remember.

Bill Neish had thought he'd found the ideal job 20 years before. After outrunning Nevada lawmen, he'd crossed into the new province of Alberta and joined the Royal Canadian Engineers to fight the Hun overseas. It seemed a nice way to say thanks for the sanctuary. Besides, didn't Canadian-born Bill Neish have an obligation to King and country?

With his military experience and a cowpuncher's feel for horseflesh, Bill was the ideal candidate for a post-war job as a Royal North West Mounted Police (RNWMP) constable. He was posted to the little town of Banff in what was then called Rocky Mountains Dominion Park. Back in the 1920s, patrolling gravel streets and muddy alleyways had been a mostly pleasant experience, although a little silly at times.

What a laugh it was standing beside your horse, looking stalwart and stern for Banff photographer Byron Harmon, or, revolver drawn, "arresting" a "bad man" on horseback, like something out of a Hoot Gibson movie.

The RNWMP had plenty of "rules and regs," and sometimes they didn't make any more sense than Harmon's poses. Bill Neish went along with them until he met his future wife. It would be years before those rules and regs allowed wedding bells to ring, so the only option was to quit the force. Doing that meant enduring the ultimate insult of buying your way out of the remainder of your hitch. Bill managed it, as others had, but it had chafed.

The warden service had its rules, too, but because wardens worked long, lone patrols most of the time, Ottawa left Bill and his colleagues in peace, as long as they kept their diaries up. Entries were terse: "Sidestepped a grizzly sow and two cubs. Warned by horse." Or "Surprised three poachers near Indian Head station." Every year wardens had to put down wapiti or bighorns thrashing in agony because ignorant city "hunters" were too lazy to go after what they wounded, or too dumb to know they had actually hit something.

Wardens agreed that one day some startled or hungry bear would kill a hiker on the trail or a store clerk in a Banff alley. Then, the "killer" would have to be killed. Some warden—maybe Bill—would lever a round into the chamber and take aim. In the backcountry, one of the lessons Bill learned was that a quick, clean kill was often a kindness.

But there was fun, too. The previous spring, riding along the Red Deer River, Bill came across warden Cliff Murphy and his wife, Nellie, who looked after 175 head of stock at the park's picturesque horse ranch, Ya Ha Tinda. How was Nellie going to get her spooky horse to cross the flooded river? Take ol' Punch, Bill offered, gesturing to his second-string horse. He's a fine swimmer; you'll be quite safe. Nellie didn't catch the wink Bill sent to Cliff, nor the grin Cliff managed to stifle. If she looked a little dubious, it was because she knew Bill's reputation as a prankster.

Ol' Punch took Nellie down deeper and deeper until the water swirled up around her waist, with Punch's head barely breaking the surface. Frantic Nellie realized the lazy beast was simply walking on the river bottom. Bill and Cliff could hear Nellie shout, "Punch, damn your rotten old hide, get out of here!" Punch got wringing-wet Nellie to the other side all right, but while the men giggled, Nellie gave Bill what-for!

Yes, Bill was having more fun than many others were having. The year before, a thousand protesters had marched through downtown Calgary, led by the Young Communist League. The police had arrested some of them, but the Communists wouldn't back down. "Release the prisoners," they told the police chief, "or we will blow your headquarters to hell!" The only thing blowing turned out to be hot air, but it made a man think. People without jobs, homes or hope—especially hope—tended to turn nasty.

Changing Times

Then, in 1932, the Depression *really* hit Alberta. Even before the war ended, times had been tough for farmers in the Dry Belt, which stretched from Lethbridge to about 30 miles east of Swift Current. Now, the hard times had hit the cattle industry as well. Desperate American ranchers persuaded Washington to close the border to Canadian cows. At the Calgary stockyards, prices dropped from seven to just two bucks per 100 pounds. The Northern Alberta Railway chugged thousands of southern Alberta families and their livestock north to Peace River homesteads. In Calgary, the Canadian Pacific Railway (CPR) closed down its shops. Businesses were going bust. Thousands of men protesting outside city hall for more work were living on relief tickets.

Banff merchants felt the difference. Mountain trips had become a luxury, and it seemed as if the CPR's great tourist days were done. If the Depression hadn't killed off rich Americans' rail excursions, eventually automobile travel would. Thirty-five-dollar-a-week bungalow camps were springing up along the new Windermere Highway. However, to the park wardens, the bad times had a good side. Let the government punch their roads through the mountains. Few people had cars, or cash to fill their gas tanks, and fewer tourists meant less trouble from handout-hungry bears. The Depression might have the entire country in its clutches, but Banff's backcountry seemed beyond its reach. For game warden Bill Neish, life went on peacefully.

2

Hot Summer

FOURTEEN-YEAR-OLD PETER WOIKEN sat at the family's large, square kitchen table, watching the flies circle lazily below the paint-peeled ceiling. Sweat trickled beneath his grimy shirt. They'd let the morning stove fire burn out, but the kitchen was already too warm. Dinner would be cold leftover chicken and the last of the previous fall's pickled beets. They still had chicken—as long as there were hens clucking in the coop—and vegetables from the garden plot that Pete's mother, Tina, kept alive with dirty washwater. As long as they had feed, the cow would give milk. Pete's father, Harry, had earned feed money on a threshing crew early the previous fall. They hoped there would be something to thresh this fall. In this corner of southeast Saskatchewan, they were lucky: 600 miles to the west, around Swift Current, things had started to get much worse. Pelly, Arran, and Kamsack were outside the boundary of the Dry Belt, although these days, it was hard to tell.

Pete's father never talked much about the weather, or about much of anything, with his four kids, but Pete was old enough now to figure some things out for himself. Standing at the screen door every morning and staring through the door's wire mesh at the cloudless sky beyond the barn, his father didn't need to say a word. Pete knew what was churning through his mind. Harry Woiken was practically willing it to rain.

Farm Boys

The fateful moment seemed to come when the well went dry at the Posnikoffs' rented farm. The Posnikoffs' own farm, located a little southwest of the Woikens' place, couldn't support George, Mary and their five kids any more. Seventeen-year-old Joe, Pete's older pal, lived on the rented farm with his brothers Fred and Harry. Pete would occasionally meet the Posnikoff brothers watering their horses at George Bush's place.

Drought or not, George said, "Sure! Bring the horses over, boys." And George shared other things besides water. Because most Doukhobors couldn't read English, he would painstakingly read letters and notices to his visitors, then write replies in English on their behalf. Families brought their sick or injured to Ida Bush, who sometimes called a doctor on their telephone, the only one for miles around. In return, grateful Doukhobors gave the owners of the semi-barren farm gifts of vegetables. Still, like other fortunate English-speakers, the Bushes got by in ways Doukhobors couldn't. Joe and Pete had heard Bush was a Justice of the Peace, which meant he could put people in jail. Bush and RCMP constable Gardener, who roomed with the Bushes, were looking for people to put in jail right now.

Somebody was burning down school houses. Most Doukhobor parents frowned and muttered, worried others would think they had burned the schools. But why would they want to do that? They practically dragged their kids into schools to learn to read and write English! However, to most people, all Doukhobors were the same, burning things down and marching around naked because they didn't like the government. In reality, the protesters belonged to just one small group, the *Svobodniki*, or Sons of Freedom.

Most *Svobodniki* had left Saskatchewan to create villages in British Columbia years before Pete and Joe were born. Most, but not all. *Svobodniki* headquarters remained in nearby Veregin, site of the burning of arms. Of course, the Sons of Freedom had torched the schools, but who could prove it? However, the *Svobodniki* were a minor nuisance compared to the more serious threats confronting every Saskatchewan farmer, Doukhobor and non-Doukhobor alike: low wheat prices and prolonged drought.

Pete wondered how long it would be before his own

father was forced to apply for relief. The unrelenting heat wave continued, withering everything in sight. The North and South Saskatchewan rivers were at their lowest level in living memory. No one, not Bush, Constable Gardener or anybody else, could do anything except wait and hope.

First Posting

Shouldering their long canvas bags, six RCMP constables strode briskly across the stone floor of Regina's cool, cavernous Union Station and out through the broad doorway to the train platform. The prairie heat hit them like an open furnace. Buttoned and belted into their uniforms, Gray Campbell and his five friends were already warm in the midday heat of late summer.

Assigned a coach coupled behind the engine, tender and a string of baggage and mail cars, they were far enough back to escape the soot wafting down from the engine's stack. Gray had learned that much travelling from Ottawa to Regina a few months before. They would ride with the windows open. There was a crucial difference between train transportation to an RCMP posting and luxury rail travel to a picturesque mountain tourist destination. An RCMP voucher entitled a constable to a coach seat, not a sleeper berth. Campbell and his buddies would doze vertically, not horizontally. At least they weren't travelling coast-to-coast. The first leg was Regina to Saskatoon, then, overnight, Saskatoon to Edmonton. By tomorrow afternoon, Constable Campbell would be saluting his OC in the city that called itself "the Gateway to the North."

Gateway it might have been, but Edmonton was still a city, not the real North of dogsled patrols, igloos, caribou and polar bears that Gray craved. In 1932, the Arctic was Canada's only remaining frontier. It had been different 50 years before, when Sitting Bull's Sioux were camped across the Great White Mother's Medicine Line. Those days had vanished almost as quickly as the buffalo. Just 34 years before, Superintendent Sam Steele and the North West Mounted Police made the Yukon safe for 30,000 Klondike gold-rush stampeders. Two years later, the gold was gone and so were Sam and the sourdoughs.

At Regina Depot, much of Gray Campbell's instruction hadn't changed since the gold-rush days: riding, rifles and revolvers, and hours of drilling on Barracks Square. Lectures on law enforcement, the Indian Act and the Criminal Code weren't much different either, nor was how easily a new recruit's name could land on a defaulters' sheet. This year, however, recruits had experienced something new.

Staring out the open window, his train click-clacking through the flat Saskatchewan landscape, Gray Campbell turned it over in his mind. The bayonets had come as a surprise, but they shouldn't have. The recruits had heard that the new commissioner, James MacBrien, was ordering them from the military. Affixing a bayonet to a rifle and learning how to use it was nothing new to Gray, after the militia. It was also nothing new to Great War veteran Lionel Broadway, the oldest constable sitting in the coach. Still, it was shocking to think of RCMP constables skewering men on bayonets, like Broadway and their fathers had done in Flanders fields. Imagine the excitement when the next lot of recruits walked into classes on machine guns and tear gas! That's what was coming, if you believed barracks scuttlebutt, and a good thing too, given the Estevan affair, which had been a terrible embarrassment for the force. Some of the guys who had faced that commie mob were likely rushed through their training and posted as fast as the six of them sitting on that train. Who could blame them if they had screwed up?

Soldiers fought wars, not policemen. Yet war was what Depot seemed to be preparing its recruits for. It was one thing when your enemy was the Hun, Fritz or the Bosche—call the wartime Germans what you wanted—but another thing when the men you fought were young Canucks like yourself, except you had a job, and they didn't. A few months ago, the idea of machine guns on the streets of Canadian cities would have seemed farfetched. However, when Regina police reinforcements arrived in Estevan after the riot, they had set up machine-gun posts throughout the tiny downtown.

Gray didn't find any of this inside the Police Officers' Manual, that little red-covered book that included everything from "Abduction: Of an heiress" to "Wounding: Peace officer." The recruits wondered: Were any of them fated to become that officer?

23

3

Market Square

AFTER THEIR ARRIVAL IN EDMONTON, Gray Campbell and the other newcomers built an outdoor corral near the detachment's substantial brick stables. They broke and trained horses brought from prairie pastures, then cantered off on long rides along the banks of the North Saskatchewan River. Before long, horses and riders were moving as one. When others arrived from Vancouver, their presence seemed to confirm that something was going to happen soon.

The Vancouver boys weren't as saddle-savvy as Gray's group, but they would have their feet planted firmly on the ground, not in stirrups. The horses learned to shoulder aside swaying sack dummies, and the newcomers acted as jeering "mobs," spooking the horses and attempting to unnerve their riot-squad riders. To outsiders, the antics of profanity-screaming constables clanking pots and waving bedsheets might have looked ridiculous, but to insiders determined to avoid another Estevan, this was serious stuff.

City Under Siege

Gray Campbell found himself in a city that, like others in western Canada, had changed enormously since 1929. The provincial capital was crowded with homeless transients. Unlike the recent RCMP arrivals, who had jobs to do and a place to live, these newcomers—a thousand souls arrived in one week alone—had nothing but the clothes on their backs and a spare set of grey underwear and socks rolled up in blankets dangling from their shoulders. At one point, fists and feet flying, destitute demonstrators fought city cops in front of the police station. Seventeen protestors were charged and thrown in the pokey, likely not protesting too much. Clean, dry and fed at the city's expense, these wanderers were probably far from delighted the day they were set free, only to be held captive by cold and hunger once again.

Bedevilled with tough fiscal choices, Edmonton resented their presence. The men the *Edmonton Journal* called "miserables" clustered inside dim, damp storm sewers directly beneath the city's struggling business centre. Police rousted the lot of them, and city crews snapped padlocks on chain-link barriers installed across the riverfront sewer outlets. Many of the evicted men didn't move far, joining others living in riverfront packing-crate shacks or in the bush east of Dawson Bridge. "Cave dwellers" burrowed into the riverbank, furnishing their semi-subterranean homes with castoffs.

Just who was responsible for housing and feeding these bums? Not us, said Mayor Dan Knott and his council, pointing their fingers east at Ottawa's Parliament Hill. Not us, insisted Prime Minister R.B. Bennett, claiming the Canadian constitution made it clear the unemployed were a local responsibility. By July 1932, both Calgary and Edmonton had stopped providing assistance for any single unemployed man, local or transient, and began sending them off to the new federal relief work camps. By the time Gray Campbell's group reached Edmonton, the hundreds who remained, as well as unemployed married men whose own "pogey" had been cut back, were growing despondent. By mid-December, plunging temperatures and nostalgic visions of Christmases past turned despondency to desperation.

Yet they kept coming. Patrolling the city's major approaches, the RCMP turned back suspicious vehicles from a score of cities, towns and hamlets. Many made U-turns and bounced into the city over rural roads. By December 20, unwilling Edmonton played host to 2,000 homeless people. Many, however, had been urged to come to the city. Constables were told it was a plot of the Communist-led Workers United League (WUL), a nefarious bunch anxious to tear down democracy's Depression-damaged defences. Just 16 years back, guys

26

like these had staged the Russian revolution, and no one should think it couldn't happen in Canada.

The WUL had persuaded the drifters to come to Edmonton, not to get relief—there was no hope of that—but to protest the fact that there was no relief. Along with other groups, the WUL was organizing a "Hunger March." Ironically, donated vegetables, meat and flour rolled in on farmers' trucks, much of it destined for the kitchen of the Ukrainian Labour Temple, not far from the city's Market Square. Debt-ridden farmers facing foreclosure were suddenly very sympathetic to the plight of the urban unemployed, seen as fellow victims of a failing economic system and hard-nosed but ineffectual politicians.

The WUL plan was to fire up the unemployed with speeches in Market Square, march them north to city hall and then straight to the provincial legislative buildings. There, on the front steps, leaders would demand a meeting with Premier John Brownlee, whose parsimonious welfare decisions seemed inspired more by big business than by the salt-of-the-earth folks who elected him. Perhaps influenced by the premier, Mayor Dan Knott and city council refused the WUL a parade permit. Would-be marchers were ordered to disperse as soon as the speeches were over.

Law-enforcement officials had a four-pronged strategy. First, they would position the RCMP's mounted riot squad across 100th Street, on the western side of the square. Second, 30 of the force's foot squad would be installed inside the square's long, one-storey Market Building. Third, city policemen would be placed on 102nd Avenue, on the square's northern side. Finally, snipers would be posted beneath the clock tower on the main post-office rooftop, in case marchers overwhelmed the police below.

A Job Well Done

Early on the afternoon of December 20, Gray Campbell and his riot-squad colleagues mounted up and took positions on 100th Street. The loudspeaker garble of hectoring speech-makers and the audience's answering applause floated over from the square. Thousands jammed the frosty grounds around the speakers' platform, and thousands more milled about on the sidewalks and spilled out onto the streets. Those on horseback realized that most weren't demonstrators but merely curious spectators out to witness the best show in town, thanks to the promotion-savvy WUL. It made little difference. The RCMP and city police were there to keep order, and anyone who disturbed that order would rue the day he came down to Market Square.

Gray's friend, little Charlie Colvin, stood quietly with others concealed inside the Market Building. For about an hour, they'd been listening impatiently to one strident speaker after another shout into the microphone a few feet away. Something had to give soon. Then, WUL committee chairman Andrew Irvine—a bigwig by the sound of it—was introduced to even wilder cheers and whistles.

"There is no law in Canada that can prevent us from walking peacefully along a sidewalk!" Irvine advised the throng. Inside the building, the officers exchanged quick glances. Was this it? "We don't want violence and I want you to refrain from violence," Irvine cautioned. "If there's any violence, let it be the police who start it." Inside the building, there were more glances. The cheeky SOB! "Now," they heard Irvine shout. "Let's go!"

The men were tense, anticipating the order to move out. "Wait for it," the NCO warned under his breath. There would be no Estevan screw-up this day, by God. There was a sudden crash. Rooftop demonstrators had dropped an enormous chunk of concrete onto a car parked in front of the Market Building, flattening it. A voice screamed over the rising voices; Mayor Knott was reading the riot act. Nobody was listening.

Gray and 21 other mounted policemen repositioned themselves a few seconds after the demonstrators reached the sidewalk on the north side of 101A Avenue. They trotted less than a block south. At the command "Squad, halt!" the horses were reined in as one. Gray saw the demonstrators wheel south onto the avenue, striding forward in pairs. "Squad, Advance!" Sergeant Baker bawled. They walked the horses calmly down the tarmac, just as they had practised. "Close up! Close up!" Baker had commanded them repeatedly during training. He didn't need to remind them now. The men moved knee to knee, a towering, nigh-impregnable wall of horseflesh and expressionless, determined riders. Slowly, they nudged the leading demonstrators, whose neat ranks began to collapse on themselves. Unable to squeeze through the line of horsemen, the demonstrators stepped back in disarray. Relentlessly, the horses moved forward, gently pushing the retreating crowd down 100A Avenue.

Then the door of the Market Building was flung open, and out poured the Mounties. Baton-wielding city police dashed across the square from the north. Hemmed in on three sides, the frustrated demonstrators flung rocks and bricks, while fur-clad Mounties and blue-uniformed city cops ducked and dodged. For the next two hours, the square became a battleground for small groups of policemen, demonstrators and mere spectators (and in this madness, what policeman on foot could tell one from the other?) clutching and grabbing, battering and bruising heads, shoulders and faces. Ducking a poorly aimed missile, Charlie Colvin took off after a pair of stone-throwing demonstrators. Through the square they fled, across 101A, twisting suddenly down an alley, the "Irish Buzzsaw" in hot pursuit. When they hit a dead end, the demonstrators took the only way out, diving through a hardware store's plate-glass window.

Up and down the avenue and then on the square itself, the troop walked their mounts back and forth, breaking up knots of cat-calling demonstrators. Gray heard a meaty smack. Slouched over his horse, Clive Holbrook shook his head and straightened up, his bloody chin wearing a rock's

Rookie constable Gray Campbell and fellow mounted riot-squad officers confront thousands of Hunger March demonstrators near Edmonton's Market Square. PROVINCIAL ARCHIVES OF ALBERTA A9025

imprint. He'd be tender for days, but he was the only riot-squad casualty. Many on foot—on both sides—were not so fortunate. Still, injuries were minor. A few hours later, police raided the Ukrainian Labour Temple and a nearby church housing the wounded, certain they would find caches of firearms. But all they found was a group of perspiring women preparing turkey dinners and unarmed men sitting at tables ready to tuck into a yuletide feast. Thirty-two men and one particularly feisty woman were arrested.

The next day, Gray and others patrolled the site of the madness the afternoon before, calmly walking their horses through the nearly deserted square. Some were calling it a riot, but Gray thought "disturbance" was a more accurate description. The Mounties felt their disciplined actions had actually prevented a riot. It was, Gray Campbell recalled, "a job well done, smoothly and efficiently."

A few days later, Gray Campbell was detailed to accompany a Ukrainian-speaking detective into the frozen countryside. Inside the detective's coat were search warrants. They were hunting for Hunger March leaders. They didn't have to look too hard; many suspects were found at family farmsteads. Campbell was surprised, but not by the truculence or even violence he had expected to encounter as young men were questioned and sometimes apprehended. Instead, he and his companion were met by parents' hearty handshakes and friendly smiles. Hot coffee was offered. Children peeked wide-eyed behind their mothers' billowing skirts. It was strange behaviour for the "criminal" class! The real leaders had vanished, and those arrested were soon acquitted.

Two months later, Calgary police apprehended WUL leader Andrew Irvine. After a violent confrontation in that city, mounted riot-squad members were hastily mustered and sent south. Calgary, however, remained peaceful. Gray and his fellow officers stayed in a makeshift dorm on the top floor of the downtown post-office building. During the day they rode sedately through city streets, making obvious eye contact with the office girls, and rode drills on the prairie.

4

Isolation

IN DEPRESSION-RAVAGED SOUTHEAST Saskatchewan, the news of a march by dozens of naked people travelled as easily as dust on the hot summer wind. Rural residents were starved for any kind of diversion in much the same way they'd been starved for a decent crop, an increase in grain prices and, more recently, three full meals a day. The zealot Sons of Freedom had taken to the roads again, but something like this might have been expected. They'd been pretty restive lately, and spiritual leader Peter P. Verigin—the very reincarnation of Christ—was back in town.

Protest on Highway 5
"We will never solve the Doukhobor problem until we get

rid of Peter Verigin," Saskatchewan premier James Anderson told newspaper reporters. The phrase "Doukhobor problem" worried those Doukhobors who distanced themselves from the radical sect. Most Canadians, including many of the Doukhobors' Saskatchewan neighbours, couldn't or wouldn't make the distinction between the Sons of Freedom and the rest. To them, every Doukhobor represented the "problem." Yet most hard-working Doukhobors lived in peace with their government and its red-coated police.

Verigin's appearance alone was enough to excite the local *Svobodniki*, but this time some regarded it as God's intervention that he was here at all. Months before, Canada had ordered the 52-year-old leader deported to Russia, from where he had fled years earlier. In the minds of many, the federal government's decision amounted to a death sentence. However, just hours before his ship was to leave Halifax, Verigin's lawyer won a reprieve. The leader had just appeared in Kamsack for a meeting, likely to choose a final destination for the Freedomites. Today, perhaps after an inspiring prayer meeting on the ground floor of Verigin's ornate home, others would unbutton their clothes and set out, eager to protest Canada's draconian government regulations.

If you were a bored teenage farm boy like 16-year-old John Kalmakoff, the prospect of seeing naked women (especially young naked women) was irresistible. If you lived near Highway 5, you hopped a bike, mounted a horse or took off on foot through the Scotch thistle—the only thing

34

that really grew on some farms anymore—hoping the cops wouldn't arrive at the scene to spoil the fun. The "scene" was just a few miles west of Kamsack, where John and his father sometimes worked at his uncle's Husky Oil depot.

The Kalmakoff farm wasn't bringing in much to live on, and lately there had been less work at Husky. While entitled to cheap, tax-free "purple" gas, farmers only reluctantly filled their tractors' tanks. If the drought continued, many wouldn't have any reason to. John missed the fun of driving the Husky truck around, making farm deliveries, but it was the pay he missed most. Maybe if he'd never shoved a five-dollar bill in his pants pocket, he wouldn't care. But now, John knew what having money meant. How were you going to get the things you wanted—snappy clothes, cigarettes, a bottle or two (the real stuff, not something distilled in someone's barn)—if your pockets were empty? How would you entice the girls?

In the meantime, here came the *Svobodniki*, trudging down the highway. The faithful were naked for a couple of reasons. Public nudity drove the rest of the population nuts. The Freedomites also believed that, being God's creation, human skin was more perfect than man-made clothes. Let them believe what they wanted, spectators snorted. It was quickly obvious that many of these people looked far better in clothes than out of them. Youthful eyes darted from marcher to marcher, searching out young, nubile figures. There were murmurs and leers at the sight of half a dozen winsome maidens who were definitely the stuff of a young guy's dreams.

In the distance, police vehicles approached, and within minutes, the stretch of highway was filled with more traffic than it usually saw during a whole week. Cars, trucks and buses skidded to a halt along the dirt shoulders. Doors thunked and voices shouted as cops arrived from every detachment for miles around. Onlookers hadn't seen this many stetsons and tunics in ages. Public nudity had recently been made a criminal offence, so the Mounties were not only instructed to break up this march before it reached Kamsack and outraged the town's good citizens, but also to transport marchers off to Yorkton for court appearances. It had become a tradition; Yorkton's magistrates had been throwing demonstrating zealots in the clink for decades.

Some of the young constables were having a good time doing their duty, or pretending to do it. One was ogling a winsome thing about John's age, not appearing anxious to load *her* into the bus. He turned and winked at a fellow officer. "Imagine, Joe," he gloated, "they're paying us for this!" His buddy, who was trying to push someone's grandmother—all 250 pounds of her—onto a bus, wasn't amused. A few minutes later, there was not a naked body in sight. The doors slammed, engines revved, gears ground, and then the buses and trucks disappeared down the highway.

It had been fun while it lasted, but when would the next excitement happen around isolated little Kamsack, Pelly or Arran? Not very soon. There was no drama in the occasional school fires. The Freedomites' slow-burning wicks were long, and by the time police arrived, another school was ashes, and the arsonists were gone. The real action was elsewhere, in Estevan and Saskatoon, where it had been the police against the poor. Anyway, torching local one-room symbols of government brainwashing made little difference to John, who had bid "good riddance" to school some time ago.

Nothing made much difference when you were poor. John suspected it was the same for farm boys or city boys. It was no different for Pete Woiken up in Arran, who was related to John by marriage, or for Pete's friend Joe Posnikoff. John liked those two, but there wasn't much fun in getting together to gripe about how tough times were. He'd had a bellyful. John decided he was going to put some money in his pocket, one way or another. He just had to figure out how.

The New Posting

Gray Campbell knew what he wanted, and it wasn't patrolling quiet downtown streets on horseback. The stultifying sameness of his Calgary duties was a constant reminder of where he really wanted to be. Still eager for the land of the Eskimo, he had volunteered for service in the Far North. If he left soon, he would still have some time outdoors before the Arctic's long, dark winter set in.

Without warning, Gray was summoned to see the sergeant in Inspector Bavin's office. Could this be what he'd been waiting for? Behind Bavin's desk, the sergeant was smiling—a good sign. After a moment came the confirmation:

Constable Gray Campbell had a new posting. But the sergeant, whose self-satisfied expression reminded Gray of someone awarding a lesser mortal a much-sought-after medal, wasn't talking about northern outposts such as Resolution or Reliance. The name Gray heard was . . . Banff?

If you worked in Calgary, you heard about Banff, but Gray's familiarity with the name went back to boyhood. Every Canadian schoolkid knew about the little tourist town nestled inside the "majestic" (the favourite modifier) Canadian Rockies. In countless newspaper advertisements, CPR brochures and colourful travel-agency posters, scarlet-coated Mounties tipped their stetsons to stylish vacationers beneath the high rock-and-timber facade of that castle-like railway hotel, the Banff Springs. Nothing Gray could imagine himself doing in tiny Banff resembled the red-blooded Mountie duties he hankered for. Thousands of boys read the likes of *Where North Holds Sway*, *Blood of the North* and other pulp-magazine Mountie adventures. The tales were tall, but their wilderness settings, where real Mountie work was done, seemed authentic enough. A ho-hum setting such as Banff would never make it between the covers of a 20-cent pulp.

"This is probably some mistake, sergeant," Gray protested. "Perhaps you could get someone else. I'm going north, so . . ." That was as far as he got. The red-faced sergeant sputtered a "you-will-proceed-where-you-are-ordered" retort. Postings were determined at the force's pleasure, not a constable's.

Isolation

The RCMP barracks at Banff, "home" to Constables Gray Campbell, George "Nipper" Combe and George "Scotty" Harrison.

WHYTE MUSEUM OF THE CANADIAN ROCKIES V113/NA2

Constable Gray Campbell had no illusions. He wouldn't be running behind a sled, mushing a team of huskies across the vast frozen wastes. Nor was it likely that he would spend his days in splendid solitude, paddling across pristine, sparkling lakes and trotting through the pines on his trusty steed. Protecting woods and wildlife was a game warden's job; police constables protected townspeople and their property.

The next day, Gray stumbled through a crowded day coach on his short train trip west. Swaying precariously

39

in the aisle, he reflected on an unexpected bit of compensation he'd learned about before boarding. His $1.50 daily wage would be, upon occasion, augmented by an extra dollar to allow him to eat outside the mess hall, as a patron of the world-famous destination's restaurants. That was an intriguing proposition.

Gray stowed his kit at Banff's station and hiked to the detachment barracks, located over the Bow River bridge and, unfortunately, in front of the Banff Zoo. Denizens of the wolf enclosure, he quickly learned, howled in response to the whistle of every passing train, day or night. Gray also learned his OC was Inspector Valentine Bruce, a former hero of the Far North whose exploits he had fantasized about, the man who had brought in the Eskimo murderers of two priests 20 years before. The constable groaned in envy. However, Gray soon discovered that envy and disappointment tended to fade away in bucolic little Banff.

Picture-Postcard Mountie

Just weeks after Gray's arrival, the summer tourist season reached its height. Mounted constable Campbell trotted off on patrols in picturesque Sundance Canyon, on Tunnel Mountain and around the golf course. He was ordered to pose with visitors alighting from Brewster Tour Packards, tallyhos and the trains that brought others, including many a lovely lady, from as far away as New Zealand and Europe.

Later, Gray and other constables took turns whirling some of these lovelies around the hotel ballroom.

The summer high life ended after the last visitors waved goodbye. On wet autumn mornings, Inspector Arthur Birch's Buick pulled the detachment's Hudson Terraplane down the road in hopes of tempting the Hudson's engine to turn over. During his month of mundane winter night patrols, Gray shuffled through the snow in silent, frigid alleyways, checking that back doors were locked up tight.

Still, Gray managed some fun. Packing skis, he and other off-duty constables climbed Mount Norquay. After a short respite at the snack shack's crackling wood-stove fire, there was the bracing hike to the summit and then the heart-pounding run down through the powdery snow and a leisurely ski back to the road and civilization. Once in a while the policemen dealt cards and poured drinks with former Mountie Bill Neish and other green-uniformed wardens, a backwoods-savvy group as tightly knit as the red-uniformed policemen. There was the occasional home-cooked dinner enjoyed with townspeople. The men took in *I'm No Angel* and *Viva Villa!* at the Lux Theatre, named for owner Norman "Mr. Banff" Luxton, the entrepreneur responsible for Banff Indian Days, which helped to bolster town commerce during the seemingly endless economic depression.

The men read about the Depression in letters and in Calgary's *Albertan* and *Herald*, and heard about it on the *Herald*'s radio station CFAC and on CFCN, which also brought them hours of religious programming each Sunday. Rotund, bespectacled Bill Aberhart broadcast *Back to the Bible* far and wide over the powerful 10,000-watt "Voice of the Prairies" station. Tens of thousands dialed 1030 to catch Bible Bill's mesmerizing Sunday sermons and hilarious skits. Inside the minister-teacher's 7th-Avenue Prophetic Bible Institute, there was almost as much politics as proselytizing going on behind the radio microphone. To laughter and applause, Bill railed at banks and mortgage companies. Aberhart had "a plan that would give you a car, a refrigerator and trips to the big city," and it wouldn't cost a dime! It was based on something he called "social credit." Many called it daft, but desperate thousands believed just the same.

Official RCMP reports chronicled Depression-inspired unrest. Dozens were injured in a bloody government-work-camp riot on the outskirts of Saskatoon as RCMP galloped into the camp to ferret out striking agitators. Struck in the head by a rock, Inspector Lorne Sampson was dragged behind his panicked horse and slammed into a post. While the battle raged, Sampson lay unconscious. He later died in hospital. Twenty-two radicals were charged. The list of western-Canadian battlegrounds grew longer. Trouble had invaded tiny Crowsnest Pass towns, where militant miners staged parades and demonstrations. Blairmore had the temerity to name a town park in honour of Karl Marx, the author of the *Communist Manifesto*.

In Banff, however, these troubles all seemed so distant.

The most tangible evidence of bad times was actually positive: Banff now had a brand-new Upper Hot Springs bathhouse. At long last, attractive timber-and-stone park gates would be a reality, and a handsome park administration building was being built. Construction crews composed of hundreds of unemployed men were housed at the nearby Healy Creek work camp. North of Lake Louise, crews from camps like the one near the tiny coal town of Nordegg were constructing a new highway between Banff and Jasper. The Mounties agreed it was a good plan to get those jobless drifters off boxcars and into camps. "Royal Twenty-centers" those men called themselves, complaining of the meagre pay of two dimes a day. But living warm and well-fed in a work camp had to be better than sleeping in a damp back alley and lining up at a soup kitchen.

For Constable Gray Campbell and warden Bill Neish, the predictable days and nights came and went, and the pleasant seasons unfolded with comforting regularity. Years later, a wistful Campbell remembered these as "golden days," when wardens and police lived in peaceful isolation, away from the depravation and despondency found on either side of the "majestic" Rockies.

5

Desperation

JOHN KALMAKOFF WOULDN'T DISCUSS his plans to get money with anyone—not even Joe or Pete—but when he actually had it, he wouldn't care how many knew. Spending his "wad" would be, unfortunately, no problem.

Mattress Money
In the fall of 1933, there were very few places where an impoverished Kamsack-area farm boy could find money. One was the row of grain elevators running along the rail siding on the west side of town. But the money paid to farmers was locked in safes. It took "soup"—nitroglycerine—to get to it. John was no safeblower. He didn't know where to get nitro, let alone how to use it. However, houses didn't

have safes. Housebreaking was a lot less glamorous than safeblowing, but it was nowhere near as risky.

John thought about a certain little log house about four miles south of Veregin, owned by Demitro Zurawell. Zurawell had been around forever; everyone knew he was rich. In case anyone needed reminding, the old farmer liked to flash a roll of bills when he went to town. John decided to visit the log house. Early Sunday morning, while Zurawell and his wife, Annie, were at church, he'd take a few gulps from a jug of nerve-steadying potato "vodka" and grab his rifle—just a young guy out early, shooting gophers.

But how was John to know Demitro and Annie wouldn't be in church that November morning, and that, instead, he would come face to face with them, right there in their own kitchen? Who would have guessed the old geezer would be such a scrapper? That Annie would go on screaming? Two quick shots, though, and they lay stretched out on the floor. He stepped over the bodies and starting looking around. It didn't take long; he yanked on the lid of a wooden trunk, and there they were—nice, fat bundles of cash. What now? Well, it didn't need to be robbery—or murder—did it? The coal-oil lamp on the bedside table smashed easily enough, and a match or two later, the soaked sheets and blankets caught nicely. Now it was just an old couple dying in a house fire. It happened all the time.

Prisoners of War

Pete Woiken tried to persuade himself that his life in

Nordegg Camp 11 was better than what he'd endured back in Saskatchewan. It was easier to do when he, Joe Posnikoff and the others sat down at the long wooden tables to eat dinner. The food was free and no worse than what was on the table back home. The clatter of cutlery seemed unnaturally loud inside the dim mess hall. The men hunched over their plates without a murmur; silence was the rule. If you broke the rule, maybe they'd cut back on food. Nobody wanted to take the chance, since the three square meals per day were the main reason they bothered to stay.

A few months later, the pot-bellied stoves would do battle with winter winds. On nearby mountains, the ridges of high, blue-white ice never melted, even in the summer sun. Come November, the bare-board walls didn't provide much protection against the wind that whipped across that frigid stuff. Everything in the camp was crude, with knocked-together bunks, tables and benches. The men had a fitting name for places like these: slave camps.

Pete and Joe's labour was muscle work—making roads and clearing brush. Their toil was made more exhausting because there was rarely a truck, 'dozer or mechanized shovel to make it go faster or easier. Those who ran the camps didn't care about that. The highway project that would connect Lake Louise with Jasper, a few miles west of the camp, would take years to complete, and most workers would never see it finished. That fact made their efforts not only mindless, it rendered them meaningless.

Others called Nordegg "prison." Dressed the same and ordered around endlessly, they felt like prisoners. Still, what crime had "jailbird" Pete Woiken committed? None that he was aware of, unless being broke and hungry qualified as a crime. It was different for light-fingered Joe, who had already done time for Calgary robberies, but you didn't have to be an ex-con to end up here. In Alberta, just being single and unemployed was enough. In Saskatchewan, when a boy turned 16, his unemployed father no longer received his share of relief. To stretch families' "pogey"—goods bought with relief—kids left home and rode "the rods," the metal crossbars fastened beneath boxcars, just inches above the track racing beneath. God help the rod-rider who fell asleep. Riding up top was safer, but Mounties and city cops were hauling men off boxcars at every stop between Vancouver and Montreal. One Calgary swoop netted almost 150 men, who disappeared into camps.

Although the camp officials dressed in civvies, smarter men than Pete weren't fooled. They said that the Canadian Army controlled the camps. Besides, word had it that the man who cooked up the camp scheme was chief of staff General Andrew McNaughton. Even the new Mountie boss, MacBrien, was a spit-'n'-polish wartime major general. So, the thinking went, if camp workers were prisoners, they were prisoners of war. It wasn't like the typical war, they were told, it was a class war, between the haves and have-nots. It was pretty obvious which side the Nordegg men were on.

Neither Joe nor Pete could read well enough to get much from *The Relief Camp Worker*, the little newspaper that new arrivals surreptitiously pulled out of their haversacks. However, you didn't need to read to understand the paper's cartoons. In one, a hard-muscled man in chains was bent over his shovel, the chains that shackled his ankles fastened around a post labelled HUNGER. At the back of his head was a revolver, levelled by a uniformed man whose high black boot bore the letters RCMP. Lying on their bunks or sitting around the table, the boys from southeast Saskatchewan listened closely as others read *The Worker* aloud. The newspaper was published by the Relief Camp Workers' Union (RCWU), dismissed by some as "a bunch of commies." Soon the RCWU had so many followers that those who disagreed learned to keep their mouths shut. Others didn't care what this bunch was called, so long as they fought for workers.

Anyone caught with *The Worker* was likely to be banished and blacklisted, every other camp declared off-limits to them. That meant no more free food and warm beds, but there was a way around that—just give the jailers running the next prison a fake name and address. Thousands of camp prisoners were now living under aliases. They wandered into camps, not at gunpoint, but forced back there by their own desperation.

By July, Joe and Pete heard mumbled bunk-bed discussions after lights-out and shared quick snatches of subversive conversation at the washhouse and inside the latrine. The word they whispered was "strike." They would make their demands clear, and those in charge had better give workers what they wanted—more pay, better clothes, books or games and maybe a phonograph and records to ease the mind-numbing monotony—or no more work. Women would be nice, too, others suggested, only half in jest. It wasn't just sex. It had been months since some had heard the sound of a woman's voice or the lilt of feminine laughter, caught a woman's heady fragrance or seen a woman's warm smile. The men laughed and then put the thought out of their minds. Thinking those thoughts wasn't healthy; it could drive a man mad.

The Nordegg men weren't the first to throw down their tools and raise their fists in western Canada. That honour had gone to the men in Saskatoon's city camp, where strikers had fought it out with the RCMP the year before. In Vancouver, the RCWU was said to be making plans, too. Yet not all strike plans went beyond brave talk. Suddenly, Nordegg officials herded the men together and issued stern warnings. Joe wondered if somebody had snitched. Was some likeable pal a police spy? Names, including Joe's and Pete's, appeared under the heading "Agitators," and the list was turned over to the all-powerful Alberta Relief Commission. Sullen and resentful, Joe and Pete were now marked men. Everyone was forced to submit before authority's threat, just like that poor stiff in *The Worker* cartoon.

Crazy Old Farmer
This business with farmer David S. Knox had turned

serious. Drumheller bailiff D.A. Oliver had no choice but to visit the boys at the RCMP. Landlord-tenant disputes were usually too trivial to involve an overworked, understaffed detachment, but now it was different. The bailiff had been uneasy from the outset, and so had Knox's landlord, who had leased him the acreage at nearby Rosebud. Knox had ignored the landlord's notice of motion to vacate.

By spring 1935, it had become a sad rural ritual. Destitute tenants unable to make rent payments or impoverished mortgagees months in arrears usually packed up their dilapidated jalopies and quietly moved on, too dejected to resist. However, almost two weeks had gone by since Knox's lease had lapsed, and he hadn't budged. Carrying a writ of possession, Oliver dutifully made the 15-mile drive west.

Knox was inside the ramshackle little house, all right. Oliver could see him through the grime-coated door window. But Oliver saw something else, too: Knox's rifle pointed directly at him. That was enough for the bailiff and the two nervous men from the cartage company contracted to carry Knox's stuff out. All three beat a hasty retreat, wagon and car jostling through the gateway at the road entrance. As he raced back to Drumheller, Oliver was still shaken by the image of the 30-30 gripped by that gaunt, unshaven old man.

Yet Knox wasn't exactly old. He had served overseas during the war, which put him in his early forties. Wounds sometimes aged a man terribly, and few were more terrible than the head wound Knox had suffered on the western front. Were the shards of metal embedded in the poor devil's skull the reason doctors had judged him mentally unbalanced years before? But these days, Oliver knew, a man didn't have to be wounded or off-kilter to age prematurely. Never-ending dust, armies of cutworms and swarms of voracious grasshoppers that ate everything, including pitchfork handles and underwear on clotheslines, created a hell that put five years on a desperate farmer for every one he survived in this drought-stricken land. Simply living a solitary existence (there seemed to be no Mrs. Knox) could turn anyone into a crazy old farmer. It was now up to the RCMP to deal with him. Much to Oliver's relief, the police decided to charge Knox, not with failure to vacate rented premises, but with unlawful use of a firearm.

The Final Visit

Ten days later, Roy Allan and another young constable named Forrest drove out to serve the summons. A few hours later, they were back at the detachment, summons in hand. When they had received no answer to calls and door-knocking, they had walked into an adjacent field where they saw Knox behind a horse plough. They called out to him. Knox deftly unhitched the horse and sent it trotting off across the furrows. Then he dashed into a coulee.

"Did you go after him?" Staff Sergeant John Skelton asked. The two constables exchanged nervous glances. The sergeant shook his head. Lord love us, these green-as-grass recruits!

The force's policy of "finishing" the recruits at their assigned detachments threatened to "finish" every exasperated OC and NCO who gave these kids their orders. Recently, the federal government had almost doubled the RCMP's budget, and Regina was churning out nearly raw recruits faster than ever. They were needed because the force had taken over the duties of provincial forces that debt-ridden governments no longer could afford. The RCMP was also the front-line defence against Canada's Communist threat, which Drumheller itself had experienced.

The Calgary Communist Party's Pat Lenihan had organized a huge march and rally in Drumheller, and the police chief had actually given him the permit. This was no secret, so the OC was able to beef up the detachment, with the questionable help of right-wing miners who opposed the Communists. More than a thousand miners shuffled into town. To no one's surprise, tempers exploded, and clubs started swinging. The constables moved aside and let the miners thrash it out among themselves. Lenihan was thrown in jail, but it didn't do much good. Drumheller residents posted his $5,000 bail—the misguided fools—putting up their homes as collateral. In the end though, Lenihan got what many thought he deserved: a year's hard labour in Fort Saskatchewan. With miners still living on the edge of poverty, tension remained high, and the police were on alert.

All of which meant that Skelton had no time for this Knox nonsense. He decided to send someone with a more take-charge attitude out to Rosebud: veteran policeman Mike Moriarity. The big, beefy, no-nonsense corporal had worn Mountie and provincial police uniforms for over a decade. Mike's orders were to take Roy Allan to the farm and, if they couldn't find Knox, simply leave the summons. After that, a no-show would mean that Mike would take the man into custody. One day before Knox's scheduled court appearance, the corporal had wedged the summons between the door and door jamb at Knox's farmhouse. When Knox failed to show up for court, Moriarity and Allan drove out to the farm once more.

Roy Allan stopped a few feet in front of Knox's gate. They couldn't just sit there by the road. They would have to pound on Knox's door and, if necessary, conduct a thorough search. They weren't leaving without him. Mike Moriarity got out of the car, walked up to the gate and swung it open. Roy drove through and stopped. Through the rear-view mirror, the constable watched Mike turn about, preparing to swing the gate shut. Then, over the soft purr of the engine, Roy heard a sharp report and saw his corporal throw his arms wide and fall to the ground.

Roy slammed the car into neutral and leapt out. More gunfire! Roy heard the thunk of slugs punching into the open door. He ducked down, using the door as a shield. Twenty feet away, Mike was stretched out on his back, blood bubbling from his mouth. Roy scrambled on his hands and knees down the rutted pathway, the crazed farmer's lead fusillade making every foot between himself and Mike seem like a mile. He dragged the wounded man to the car's rear door as more shots ricocheted around them. Trembling in fear and panting from exertion, Roy reached for the door handle. Bent double, he propped the open door steady with his hind end. He now had two shields between himself and the farmhouse. If only he could stay below the windows.

Mike was semi-conscious, clearly unable to crawl onto the back seat. Somehow, Roy had to lift him up and onto the floor between the seats. Stretching him out neatly on the backseat was out of the question. Roy heaved Mike up against the door ledge—the guy weighed a ton! Another shot crashed out. Speed was all that was going to save them now. In the next few seconds, Roy managed to wedge Mike between the seats and slam the rear door shut, the injured man's legs folded up behind it like an accordion. In his mind, Roy was already racing down the gravel road toward—where? Did Rosebud have a doctor?

Roy was about to crawl in behind the wheel when Knox fired again. The driver's door window exploded. Roy turned away as the spraying glass bit into his forehead and cheek. Mike wasn't the only one bleeding now, but at least Roy could still see. He slammed the car into reverse and roared through the gateway, screeched to a halt on the road, and then, wheels spinning and engine screaming, tore away.

6

Drumheller Standoff

RCMP INSPECTOR ERNIE BAVIN SLAMMED down the telephone receiver and strode out of his office. There'd been a shooting out near Drumheller, he announced. Constable George "Nipper" Combe stared wide-eyed at the inspector. More experienced officers than the young, two-year constable showed respectful interest, but a shooting was no longer breathtaking news. Gunplay and other violence had become a habit on the prairies, especially in Alberta.

Violent Times
Almost four years before, near Pincher Creek, a suddenly destitute farmer shattered by crop loss took a lethal drink of formaldehyde. A month later, in Camrose, less than an hour

west from where Combe was sitting, the local lumberyard manager lost his job. He went home, shot and killed his wife and two daughters and then drowned himself in a nearby lake.

A week or two after that, three hours north of Edmonton, someone else who had lost everything shot his old folks and then turned his rifle on himself. That August, Lethbridge police corralled an unemployed transient and locked up the noisy nuisance overnight. By morning, he was dead, having somehow managed to commit suicide. A few months after the jail-cell suicide, Lloydminster's Harold Huxley killed himself over financial difficulties. The entire province was stunned. Transients and destitute farmers, sure, but the city's long-time mayor?

It was the same in Saskatchewan. There was the sad case of Gannett Bissett, a farm worker charged with vagrancy. Like hundreds of others, he spent 30 days in the Regina lock-up. Bissett left his jail cell alive but didn't stay that way for long. Back home in Cabri, living on relatives' charity, he killed himself with a .22 rifle. The worst example of deadly desperation was a hapless couple named Bates. Making a suicide pact, they drove to a deserted schoolyard near Biggar with their eight-year-old son, Jackie. There they waited for the car exhaust's carbon monoxide to carry them peacefully away. But it seemed Bates had about as much success with suicide as he had as a butcher or businessman. The car ran out of gas. The two finally woke up, but poor Jackie didn't. "Do something! Finish me off too!" Bates' distraught wife begged. He tried knocking her on the head with the engine crank, then switched to a butcher knife and, finally, a penknife, which he also tried on his own wrists. Both survived and were arrested for murder.

Then, just a few months back, there was the case of a farmer's wife south of Camrose. For some reason, Isabel Brown attempted to kill her six children with candies laced with gopher poison. Thankfully, only one of them died, but before he did, relatives pounded on the barricaded bedroom door, urging Isabel to come out and at least bid her dying little boy a fond farewell. Her only response was a blast from the rifle she used to kill herself.

So "There's been a shooting" didn't explain the inspector's grim demeanour. Then it came: this was no self-inflicted wound. Worse, the man shot was one of their own. It was the kind of news a Mountie never wanted to hear. For a second or two the room went still. Was it always that way when a fellow officer got it? Nipper didn't want to ask. Given the recent epidemic of violence, it was only a matter of time before another Mountie became a victim, like Inspector Lorne Sampson in Saskatoon. The unspoken question hung in the air: "Is he . . . ?" Bavin shook his head; he didn't know.

The man shot was Michael Moriarity, a corporal at the Drumheller detachment. If others in the office had known of Bavin's link with the victim, they would have quickly understood the inspector's uncharacteristic emotional reaction to the news. Back in 1922, during a Crowsnest Pass rumrunning and murder investigation, Moriarity had served under Bavin when both men wore the uniform of the Alberta Provincial Police. Moriarity questioned and then took custody of suspect Florence Lassandro, destined to be the last woman hanged in Alberta. The man whom Florence or rumrunner Emilio Picariello had shot and killed was a police constable. Now, in the cruellest kind of irony, Bavin's duty was to help to bring Moriarity's own assailant to justice. However, someone else in the room also had a close connection with Moriarity. The corporal's name hit Nipper Combe like a fist driven into his solar plexus. Just a few months before, Moriarity had shaken Nipper's hand and wished him well on his transfer from Drumheller to Calgary.

Then, incredulity set in. An RCMP officer shot in little ho-hum Drumheller? What was more, it hadn't actually happened *in* Drumheller, but at some nearby rural crossroads named Rosebud. The inspector was very specific about the location. He'd been asked to get some men out there; the gunman was still at large. Bavin pointed a finger at the man in charge of the Calgary section, Sergeant Jack Cawsey. Cawsey pointed at a couple of others and then at Constable Combe. Nipper had a hunch that Cawsey had included him because of his personal connection with Moriarity. Then, a more practical reason suggested itself: he was probably the only one who knew a quick way to Rosebud.

Missed Opportunity

Within minutes, the group was on the highway. Combe's

mind skipped from question to question. What would he see? Would he be in the line of fire? Meanwhile, the sergeant behind the wheel seemed frustrated to the point of anger. As they sped east, Jack Cawsey explained why: he hadn't had time to get his dog.

Before he was transferred to Calgary from his tiny one-man detachment at the railroad hamlet of Bassano, Jack Cawsey had speculated about the role canines might play in search and apprehension procedures. He took a dog along when he made patrols through CPR property looking for trespassers and transients. Cawsey was struck by the untrained animal's eagerness to jump into freight cars—sometimes 50 a night—and his apparent ability to search them. If a dog was properly trained, what might he be able to do? Then, in 1933, Cawsey purchased a young German shepherd he named Dale. Before long, Dale had answered Cawsey's question. When he did, the RCMP, which had encouraged Cawsey's experiment, offered the sergeant 25 cents a day to keep Dale (a pittance, Cawsey grumbled), on the condition Dale would be available for duties anywhere in K Division, which meant the entire province of Alberta.

Dale could find a cold trail, track down a fugitive and hold him. Over a distance of a mile, through fields and across irrigation ditches, the dog could discover evidence and return those articles. He could climb a ladder and scale a 10-foot fence. Who knew what else he might be capable of? Because men's lives were in danger, there wasn't time for

Cawsey to drive out to the dog's kennel on the outskirts of town. Yet Cawsey knew that a well-trained police dog could protect the men he worked with, and what better proof could there be than his performance in a dangerous manhunt exactly like this one?

The Granary

By the time Combe and other RCMP officers arrived in Rosebud, the manhunt was over. Police and local volunteers had cornered the fugitive inside an empty granary, more than four miles from where he had shot down Moriarity. The new arrivals also discovered that Corporal Moriarity was dead.

There was scarcely time for a round of handshakes and brief commiseration with the bandaged Roy Allan before Knox opened fire on them again. Drumheller police, farmer-volunteers and visitors hunkered down behind cars and trucks. The standoff had been going on for almost two hours, which was too long for Staff Sergeant John Skelton's liking. The afternoon light was going fast. If they were still out here once darkness fell, Knox could simply slip away.

A voice shouted, "He's out!" and the policemen peered cautiously around fenders. Knox, little more than a dim, grey smudge on the horizon, took cover behind a haystack a few paces from the granary. Gunfire erupted from the police and volunteers. When the smoke cleared, there was nothing much to see but the haystack and the granary. Had Knox darted back inside the building? There was only one way to know for sure; somebody had to come up on the gunman from behind. However, stumbling around in semi-darkness was dangerous, especially if Knox swung that rifle around.

Constable Richard Fenn, from little Irricana, offered to drive around, arguing he would get there fast and keep low. Skelton nodded. Hoping to distract Knox, the police kept up a steady fire until Fenn disappeared. Then, with Fenn approaching from behind, they didn't dare keep shooting. "Hey, look!" someone shouted. The men peered up the rutted road. The rifleman was out in the open, kneeling beside the haystack. Had they hit him? It was hard to know. Then he fell face down.

Crouched behind the wheel, Fenn was so close—his head mostly below the dashboard—that all he could see through the windshield was part of the haystack. Where was Knox? There was an ominous thump and the car bounced. Fenn had rolled over something. He stomped the brake pedal and opened the door cautiously, using it for cover. Glancing around the door, he saw men, guns at the ready, dashing up from the road below. Looking down, he saw Knox lying with his legs beneath the car and torso stretched out toward the blood-splattered siding of the granary.

What If?

Knox was dead, but how exactly had it happened? He had obviously suffered a grievous head wound. Bad light, distance and obstructed vision fuelled speculation as Combe, Cawsey and the rest stared down at the dead farmer.

The story in that night's *Calgary Herald* was laughable. The local "reporter" (someone from the *Drumheller Mail*?) must have scrambled to make the paper's deadline, and it showed. Initially referred to as "corporal" (correct) in charge of Drumheller detachment (incorrect), Moriarity was demoted to "constable" just a few lines later. Knox, readers learned, "pulled a revolver out of his pocket" to kill Moriarity. That was pure bunk. There was worse; the *Herald* reported that Fenn crushed Knox against the granary with his car, a "fact" met with derision by those who were there.

However, speculation about other details continued, Nipper learned, when members of the hastily assembled coroner's jury questioned Fenn, Skelton and others about the events. Skelton was adamant that Fenn did not kill Knox with his car. Crouched down on the road, how could the staff sergeant be so sure? Nipper was just a few feet away from Skelton, and he wasn't certain. Neither was Fenn, but he said little; Skelton did the talking. The jury concluded Knox was likely already dead when Fenn rolled over him. Nobody wanted to argue that point. Knox, therefore, was killed by a bullet. But from whose weapon?

The jury concluded it came from Knox's Winchester. That raised some eyebrows. Could Knox's arms have reached far enough for his finger to nudge the trigger of a long-barrelled 30-30 rifle? The jury speculated that, surrounded and unable to escape, Knox had put a bullet into his own brain. After killing one Mountie, wounding another and holding off more than a dozen, did Knox suddenly develop a guilty conscience? In any case, he could easily have avoided suicide by simply stepping out in plain view—which he did—and let someone else's bullet end his life. However, nobody seemed anxious to question the jury's conclusion.

As the days passed, there was another kind of speculation. Why did this quiet and unassuming guy, according to neighbours, turn killer? That was easy to answer, some argued: finances. Weren't the landlord, the bailiff and the police all trying to throw him out of house and home? But when they went through Knox's pockets, police found a roll of bills worth $300, more money than most farmers would see that year or the next. Others contended that Knox's head wasn't right. Shrapnel embedded in his skull from someplace "over there" had finally unhinged him.

The jury's finding of suicide allowed higher-ups to quickly close the book on the case. Nobody wanted to suggest that upright Mounties had shot down a troubled, lonely farmer who also happened to be a disabled First World War vet—a suggestion that bleeding-heart commies would certainly pounce on. The rank-and-file could stop gnawing it over too. The last thing the RCMP needed was young, impressionable constables burdened with guilty consciences; there was too much of that already, after Estevan and Saskatoon. It was time to push on.

7

On to Ottawa

JOE POSNIKOFF TRUDGED SILENTLY down the highway. A few feet behind, his buddy Pete Woiken kept an amiable silence. They were just east of Banff, ears cocked for the sound of a vehicle that signalled a potential ride.

During their last few days at Nordegg, all they had heard was "Get out." When the strike plans were dashed, a lot of the men simply lost heart. "Let us go forward in the coming struggle with the only weapon that gets results, organized militant action!" *The Worker* had urged, but the stirring words lost their power after the strike plans were uncovered. Through the long, grey winter months, despondent men were reduced to thinking it was every man for himself. Joe felt that way, too. Then, new guys from BC showed up.

It was a province-wide strike, newcomers crowed; thousands from more than 50 work camps had flooded into Vancouver. Over $5,000 had been collected from sympathetic downtown pedestrians. The RCWU leader, limping "Slim" Evans—a lean, handsome guy who had stopped a machine-gun bullet in a Colorado strikers' riot—actually asked city police to guard the cash ("Moscow Gold," he told them, cheeky devil!) until the bank opened. In Stanley Park, 300 moms formed a human Valentine's heart around 1,000 strikers. There was no mistaking the strikers' sentiment. Huge placards read "Abolish the Work Camps."

The strike was just the prelude. Somebody—nobody remembered who—came up with a brilliant idea: take the men's demands straight to Ottawa. Strikers would travel on top of CP boxcars, the same way thousands of others had. They called it the "On-to-Ottawa Trek." Hundreds were ready to march on Parliament Hill.

The only way the Nordegg workers were going to haul their asses onto that train was to get out of camp. So, during the first days of June 1935, they defected, not only from Nordegg, but from camps near Edmonton, Jasper, Banff, Kananaskis and Calgary. Some just quietly disappeared, reportedly last seen going to the latrine, on work detail or leaving mess hall after dinner. Others, eager to face off against authorities, ignored wake-up or refused to pick up tools. If supervisors didn't like it, they could shove it. Agitators got walking papers fast, along with the usual dire threats of blacklisting. Would-be trekkers merely jeered. When Joe, Pete and dozens more hit the road this time, they had a specific destination: the Stampede City.

Calgary Hospitality

The long, 50-car freight train hissed to a stop at the 10th Street West crossing. Hundreds of unshaven, grimy men crouched on boxcar catwalks turned stiffly this way and that, rubbernecking—few of them had ever seen Calgary—but most just sat, arms around knees, wondering where the railyards were. Below, a small group of curious residents realized that the men were waiting for orders. Their obvious discipline surprised onlookers. At trek marshall Jack Cosgrove's command, hundreds obediently climbed down. Then, just like an army, they shuffled about, forming up in three divisions, four abreast. Under the watchful eyes of division captains and platoon corporals, the trekkers began marching through downtown Calgary to the only place big enough to house them all: Victoria Park, site of the famous Calgary Stampede. A single bemused motorcycle cop puttered about the long procession, as if escorting the Stampede Parade, minus the bands and floats, rather than the biggest anti-government demonstration in Canada's history. The smiling spectators on sidewalks and leaning out of second- and third-storey windows applauded, called out and sent up scattered cheers.

Trek leaders learned it was no accident that the On-to-Ottawa train stopped where it did. The crossing was within sight of the towers and turrets of the Mewata Armouries. Inside that medieval-looking monstrosity, a unit of the famed Lord Strathcona's Horse was mustered, preparing to ride out against them. The steel-helmeted soldiers were awaiting the order from the provincial government in Edmonton to mount up and move out. The order never came.

The men were billeted inside the cavernous grandstand building, courtesy of city council, which nevertheless refused them soap, towels, bedding or food since none of them had lived in the city for the required six months. A few yards from the grandstand, dozens stepped into the cool shallows of the Elbow River to wash away soot and grime. Everyone was given 15 cents apiece for meals at nearby cafés. For new arrivals such as Joe and Pete, it was a meagre start, but word got around that smooth-talking organizer Matt Shaw, who got himself on CFAC before the train even arrived, was on the air again, asking for food and clothing.

The very next day, Joe, Pete and hundreds more were on the streets conducting a tag day. Calgarians didn't care that the men had no permit. Nickels, dimes and quarters dropped into the tin cans, and when the counting was done, just over $1,300 worth of critical donations was tallied. Yet, even this significant amount didn't truly reflect Calgary's sentiment. "Tin-canners" were greeted with smiles instead of sneers, laughter instead of threats and warm pats on the back instead of the punches they expected to take. The two Saskatchewan farm boys were scarcely able to believe it.

Hold the fort, for we are coming! An army of the unemployed, the On-to-Ottawa trekkers march through downtown Calgary toward Victoria Park, home of the Calgary Stampede. GLENBOW ARCHIVES NA-4532-1

Curiously, both the Calgary City Police and the despised RCMP were conspicuous by their absence.

However, with hundreds arriving from various camps, the money wouldn't go far. When police stood back during the tag day, organizer George Black upped the ante. Later that afternoon, trekkers laid siege to the offices of the Alberta Relief Commission on Seventh Avenue. "We want food! We want food!" hundreds chanted. Bemused Saturday shoppers watched dozens snake-dance rhythmically around the former telephone building. Organizers barged inside and commission chairman A.A. Mackenzie was "taken hostage." Since the trekkers were not Albertans, the chairman argued he had no authority to provide assistance. Trek leaders told Mackenzie they were prepared to wait as long as he was prepared to go hungry. The trekkers would outlast him; they'd been hungry more often than he had. Two hours later, Mackenzie caved in and agreed to provide funding for two meals a day for the next three days. Down on the street, trekkers greeted the news with a triumphant cheer.

That night, the rally at the Stampede grounds took on a celebratory air, with boyish Matt Shaw addressing over a thousand Calgarians. In a lively speech punctuated by cheers and applause, Shaw explained the reasons behind the BC strike and the decision to go to Ottawa. Some of the guys were sure they were making history. Joe or Pete didn't know about that; they only knew how good they felt being part of the trek and headed somewhere (not to mention being fed and housed along the way). For the moment, that was enough, and it was more than they had dreamed of.

The next day, close to a thousand trekkers marched across an iron bridge to picturesque St. George's Island, striding up the dirt entranceway beneath twin rows of globe-topped lamp standards, past trimmed lawns and tidy flower beds showing early-summer colour. Hundreds of residents pressed forward for handshakes, opening wicker hampers brimming with home-cooked food. Near the two-storey teahouse, a concert band struck up, and kids ran around, laughing with delight. Meanwhile, there were many questions:

"Good reception from the folks back in BC?"

"Pretty cool in Kamloops; Revelstoke wasn't much better."

"What was it like coming through the mountains?"

"Them spiral tunnels were some kind of hell! Over and over, a blast of heat that fixed to fry your brains, smoke so thick you couldn't breathe."

"Where's home, son?" How long had it been since these guys, some as young as 15, had been called "son?" For some, there was no love lost for family, but the more others talked about home, the more they missed it. Residents regarded them affectionately, seeing their own sons, nephews and cousins in the faces of the trekkers.

Then the subject of the camps came up, and the scrubbed, fresh-faced folks wanted to hear it all: What was the food like? How could risking everything on the trek be better than camp? They didn't beat you or anything, did they? Joe and Pete tried to answer, but words didn't come easily like these nice people seemed to expect. When they spoke, it was like a door slammed shut, leaving the Calgarians inside and the boys standing outside. Aha, Russians, Ukrainians, bohunks! Smiles froze in place, and eyes shifted away.

Later that night, at the stadium, there was a trekkers-only rally to welcome 150 Edmonton newcomers. Waving a piece of paper, program chair Red Walsh explained that he had received a note from a group of Calgary ladies. The women wanted to ease the loneliness of the men, Walsh read; they would find a woman for every man on the trek! Laugher erupted. Walsh was eager to seize the moment, "All right! Let's put it to a vote!" With a show of hands, and a newfound sense of pride and purpose, the trekkers regretfully turned down the offer.

A Revolutionary Movement

Three hours' drive west, officers inside Banff RCMP barracks read the *Calgary Herald* and *Albertan* with disgust bordering on dismay. Why hadn't police cracked down on those so-called trekkers? Maybe panhandling without a permit was a wink-and-nudge offence, but that hostage-taking at the Alberta Relief Commission office was something else again. With no help from police, no wonder Mackenzie had capitulated. Under the circumstances, what choice did he have? The whole episode was shameful.

And the tone of the stories! Newspapers and readers had clearly fallen in love with those louts. "Tourists," the papers called them. Living and working in Banff, Gray Campbell and his pals knew all about tourists, and this shiftless bunch certainly didn't qualify. For one thing, they were all broke; for another, far from supporting the community, as real tourists did, these parasites were doing the opposite. They had taken over $1,300 out of residents' pockets and hundreds of dollars from the Alberta Relief Commission. Instead of giving those bums the cold shoulder, what had Calgarians done? Invited them to a picnic! The fact that they were Communist-led seemed irrelevant. Even an *Albertan* editorial confessed, "To be quite frank, we don't care very much."

A Calgary resident had even told a reporter, "When we saw how orderly and well behaved they were, everyone warmed up to them." Those sly commies! It was enough to make any self-respecting law officer puke. Following this perverted logic, if the trekkers were the "good guys," then the "bad guys" were anybody in a uniform.

To the Mounties, the lack of action was perplexing. Less than three years before, Gray and the others had been sent to Calgary on the strength of their success at Edmonton. Hadn't the Hunger March taught them anything? If policemen living and working inside a little mountain-resort enclave were frustrated, how must those inside the Calgary police station have felt, powerless to stop events unfolding all around them? What was Inspector Bavin thinking?

Gray Campbell's frustration would have deepened if he'd known of the inaction that greeted the warning sent by Bavin to Saskatchewan's assistant commissioner, Colonel Stuart Wood. "There would be serious consequences unless action were [sic] taken to stop the trek," Gray's former OC wrote. He had no doubt that the On-to-Ottawa Trek was "clearly a revolutionary movement." However, as Wood put it, police did not have "sufficient strength to deal with the situation." Either forgetting—or ignoring—Lord Strathcona's Horse, Wood reported the combined city and RCMP contingent numbers at just 90 men. Gray Campbell would have gnashed his teeth, recalling how 22 mounted men, 30 RCMP officers and a few dozen city policemen dispersed a huge throng of over 8,000 in Edmonton's Market Square, without the loss of a single life.

The very evening Bavin wrote to Wood, over 2,000 smiling well-wishers saw the trekkers off as the freight train got up steam. Kindly CPR trainmen helped the men up onto the boxcars. The "revolutionary movement" of fewer than 1,200 men was set to roll again.

When the On-to-Ottawa Trek shuddered to a stop at Medicine Hat, everyone was in a foul mood. Joe was angry at himself; this wasn't his first time hooking a drag. He and Pete had ridden the rails from Saskatchewan to Alberta and learned plenty in the hobo jungles. What those 'boes knew! "Next through freight east is 404, hauled by engine No 3554, gonna be made up on track number 12," and the exact departure time, too. Would the bulls raid the stiffs that night? Someone sitting around the little fire would have an answer: "Too many of us for them to clip us tonight." Nods and murmurs: hobo jungle wisdom.

Dampened Spirits

Sitting in a camp for so long, Joe had forgotten that wisdom. A stiff wind came up, driving the rain across them all. Before they had rolled many miles, everyone was drenched and frozen to the bone. After the night they'd endured, Medicine Hat offered them sandwiches and coffee. Joe watched the cheering men lunge for the tables, Pete included, as if this was the greatest feast ever. Joe joined in; he was as ravenous as the rest, but his gnawing hunger only fed his anger. It shouldn't have been this way, after the rousing send-off Calgarians had given them, complete with food, blankets and clothing—thanks to Matt Shaw. Joe respected Shaw for that. Matt was right at home on the speakers' platform or inside those almost-magical places called radio stations. Now, there were too many bosses and too many orders.

They had been marching to the train in the new fourth division made up mostly of Joes and Petes from camps all over Alberta. The street was jammed with applauding Calgarians, including the young, curvy kind. No guy Joe knew—including little Pete, who had an eye for a nice thing in a skirt—was going to ignore an opportunity when folks thought he was a hero. There were nudges and laughter when some horny guy made a quick dash over to the sidewalk, "Hi, there, honey! Wanna go on a train ride with me?" Within seconds, others were exchanging happy talk, getting in a quick squeeze or two. Then some spoilsport screamed, "Get back into line, you lot! Get back, now!" That wasn't the end of it, though. Once at the train, other divisions were quickly dismissed, but not the fourth.

"What the hell's goin' on here?" barked a rigid little guy named Paddy O'Neill, as he strutted back and forth in front of them. "Have you bastards gone mad?"

O'Neill's strident voice flipped a switch, and Joe's

breathing quickened. "Do you think we've spent years building our organization to have you come and wreck it?" O'Neill ranted. There was more, but the blood roaring in Joe's ears drowned out his words. He wanted to elbow his way to the front and punch the jerk in the face. Joseph Posnikoff hadn't come all this way to be yelled at and ordered around like he was still in Nordegg. Maybe it was time to get off this damn train, too. He wouldn't be the first one to hit the road again on his own. New men had joined up, but the trekkers' numbers hadn't grown since Kamloops, more than a week before, so what did that tell you?

The Queen City

The trek rolled on. Swift Current came and went, followed by Moose Jaw, where there was another rally and more fighting words directed to police. Matt Shaw shouted, "If they attack us, we are not going to lay down and take it!" And, as if to test their endurance, the rain poured down.

Just before sunrise on Friday, June 14, the wet, exhausted trekkers rolled into Saskatchewan's capital. There they heard the bad news: they might not roll out again. According to newspapers, the federal government had decided the On-to-Ottawa Trek would end right there. To make sure, the RCMP had beefed up its Regina detachment with a riot squad from nearby Depot Division. The *Saskatoon Star Phoenix* called the decision "an inexcusable and unforgivable Hitlerian action."

It's the federal government, other trekkers told Joe and

Pete, led by pompous Prime Minister R.B. Bennett—R.B. stands for "Rotten Bastard." Now Joe understood why the folks back home called their horse-drawn cars and trucks "Bennett Buggies." The pathetic rubber-tired "wagons" were proof of R.B.'s broken promises about jobs and better times. Sure, R.B.'s government was the enemy, but fat, flabby politicians weren't on the front lines. Trekkers had some thoughts about the police too: Government sees us comin'? They unleash the Mounties like a packa hounds! Come to think of it, didn't the czar have somethin' like the RCMP, too, Joe? Cossacks! Ridin' down the poor peasants, swords swingin', just like Mounties, swingin' their billy clubs.

However, when Joe, Pete and the rest climbed down from the boxcars, there wasn't a Mountie in sight. Trek leaders were met instead by the hard-working representatives of the Citizens' Emergency Committee. Regina had it all planned. In a few hours, there would be a mass rally at their temporary Exhibition Stadium home. The next day, Saturday, would be a tag day, and on Sunday there would be a picnic, so the public could meet the boys. There would be free movie tickets and boxing and wrestling matches. Pete was excited, and even cynics like Joe decided to wait and see what would happen before taking off. Reaching Arran would be quick and easy, but the thought of going back gave Joe no comfort. Besides, if there was going to be a fracas with the cops, he wanted in on it.

That evening, Regina did Calgary one better. Over

6,000 residents, many arriving by special streetcar service, filled Exhibition Stadium to hear Matt Shaw, George Black and hometown organizers speak in a rousing three-hour rally. A CKCK microphone stood on the platform, and those unable to attend had tuned in. Slim Evans wound it up in fine style, announcing that, "There are not enough Cossacks in the Dominion to stop us, if the workers unite in saying, 'Hands off the Relief Camp Strikers'!" Many resolutions were passed, including one demanding that the prime minister remove all obstacles in the way of the trekkers' journey to Ottawa.

The climax came when 1,200 trekkers stood as one to cheer Queen City residents. They had much to thank them for. Just hours before, tag-day efforts had netted almost $1,500, surpassing even Calgary's generosity, and this in a city where one out of every five citizens was on relief. At the picnic, where 5,000 residents (an estimated 10 percent of the city's population) mingled with trekkers, there was even more reason to be grateful. Bakeries donated hundreds of loaves of bread, cookies and doughnuts; grocery outlets contributed meat, cheese and gallons of lemonade, coffee and tea. And there were girls, too!

Change of Plans
On Monday, June 17, the trekkers were ready to roll east again at 10 p.m. Leaflets urging Regina citizens to see the boys off had blanketed the city. But there were disturbing rumours swirling about. Would the police be there to keep

them off the boxcars? Then, more news came: the government had sent out a couple of cabinet ministers to negotiate with the trekkers. Pete was puzzled. What did "negotiate" mean? He didn't ask; there was no point in looking stupid. He listened closely and soon got the gist of it. But why all the talk about what the trekkers wanted? It was obvious: they were going to Ottawa! Paddy O'Neill had told the crowd at Moose Jaw, "We are going through with the march and we don't care if we have to go in our stockinged feet!" Were they changing their minds? Pete couldn't get much out of Joe, who angrily brushed off his questions. Then Pete and Joe learned they wouldn't be marching to their train after all.

Later that night, perched on a truck bumper in front of the men, Evans bawled out the terms agreed to by the government: a seven-man delegation was off to Canada's capital. Any offer would be brought back for the trekkers' approval. In the meantime, there would be three meals a day for the men, better sleeping accommodation and no interference whatsoever from police. "This is a tremendous victory for us," Evans shouted. Pete glanced at Joe to see his reaction, but Joe's impassive face revealed nothing.

"All in favour?" Evans shouted.

The crowd yelled back, "Aye!"

"Opposed?" There was a brief silence.

"Bennett!" some wiseacre squeaked. The men roared with laughter. Guffawing with the rest, Pete looked over at Joe and his heart leapt; his friend was laughing as loudly as he was.

By the time the trek delegation arrived back in Regina from Ottawa one week later, no one was laughing. Bennett had blithely dismissed the trekkers' demands. Back to the camps, you bunch, summed up his stance. Evans' outraged reaction had reached Regina days before he stepped down from the train at Union Station. As the delegates' train crawled westward, Evans met the press in every town, telling the tale of deceit and betrayal at the hands of R.B. Bennett, who looked, Evans sneered, "like a great, overfed toad."

All around Pete and Joe, speculation ran wild. Is it true they're setting up a new camp especially for us? Damn right, others nodded, they've got the guys from Dundurn Camp pitchin' tents and stringin' barbed wire right now near Lumsden.

Surely Regina people would help them out again, as they had just a few days before? But the *Leader-Post* suggested otherwise: "If marchers should attempt to defy constituted authority, Regina citizens must then take up their stand on the side of law, order and the authorities who hold office." The town, it seemed, was turning against them, caving in to that overfed toad in Ottawa. The CPR, once an ally, was now going to enforce the federal Railways Act that made the trekkers trespassers. As a result, trek leaders decided that if they couldn't use the rails, they would use the roads.

A test run was staged to see what, if anything, police would do on Highway 1. On Thursday night, June 27, trekkers stood in division formation on the grass in front of Exhibition

Stadium, watching a chosen few jump up onto a flatbed truck and squeeze inside a couple of cars. Within their ranks, a bespectacled, academic-looking trekker named Marsh pumped out chords on the squeezebox strapped around his shoulders. Those chords were the cue to belt out the revised lyrics of an old hymn they had adopted as their anthem. Pete and Joe shouted the words along with the rest:

> We meet today in Freedom's cause,
> And raise our voices high;
> We'll join our hands in union strong,
> To battle or to die.
>
> Hold the fort, for we are coming; union men, be strong.
> Side by side we battle onward,
> Victory will come!

Doors slammed and engines revved. About 25 trekkers and their volunteer drivers headed off into the twilight toward the highway: "Hold the fort, for we are coming." An hour later, when the vehicles stopped to fill up at a highway gas station, dozens of Mounties in riot gear poured out of rented cartage vans. Those trekkers who didn't flee into the crowd of jeering, booing spectators were hustled away for questioning, along with the good-hearted volunteers.

CHAPTER

8

Riot City

SUBDUED BY THE HIGHWAY DEBACLE, Evans and his leaders concluded they had to negotiate with the authorities. The only way they could do that effectively was if the trekkers set up their own camp; they were too vulnerable in the stadium. Joe scoffed. It looked like he and Pete had traded one camp for another. A few had already registered for Lumsden. All a guy had to do was walk into the nearby World Grain Show Building. Joe vowed he wouldn't do that. He'd hit the road before he walked into anybody's camp.

The Last Rally

On the evening of Friday, July 1, Pete Woiken, Joe Posnikoff and a few hundred others marched over to Regina's Market

Square for a rally. It was the Dominion Day holiday, but otherwise, nothing special. This was the third time the trekkers had gathered on the dusty downtown site. What were they going to hear that night that they hadn't heard before? Probably nothing. That fact, and worries about eviction from the stadium, kept hundreds at the exhibition grounds watching baseball. The rally wasn't really for trekkers, anyway; it was aimed at Regina residents. Trekkers needed their support to finance their proposed camp. At least the rain had held off, and it was a pleasant evening as trekkers mingled with hundreds of Regina families.

The fact that the square's south end faced the city's police station across the street had not gone unnoticed. Now, as trekkers stood before the flatbed truck that served as a dais, listening to yet another plea for donations, third-division leader Steve Brodie noticed something else. "Look what is here!" he murmured to one in his division, nodding at a parked moving van on the street behind the speakers. "I can smell trouble."

Joe followed Brodie's gaze and saw the van's rear doors swing open. He gave Pete a hard nudge. Pete craned about, and his eyes widened. Steel-helmeted cops, dozens of them, were filing out of the van and lining up along the sidewalk.

"If there's no trouble," Brodie's companion murmured, "then *they* are going to bring it."

There were more nudges and whispers. Trekkers watched across the square as RCMP officers in riot gear strode off another van. Fingers pointed to the north end, where a third van was parked. Moments later, a police whistle cut the air, signalling the start of a terrible ordeal that trekkers and spectators alike would never forget.

The Streets Run Red

Slack-jawed trekkers saw spectators at the square's south end scatter. Spilling out of their station, dozens of blue-jacketed city police, wielding what look like sawed-off baseball bats, dashed straight for the speakers' platform. Anyone in their path was knocked flat. Joe's mouth moved, but Pete couldn't hear a word; the air was filled with an almost inhuman roar. The RCMP advanced into the square from the other three sides, swinging their batons at anyone—old, young, male, female—not quick enough to scramble away.

Close by, four cops beat a striker curled up at their boots, his arms shielding his head from their clubs. "Murder!" a woman screamed. A snarling policeman turned and whacked the woman across the knee; she dropped like a stone. Pete stood dazed by the mayhem. Joe dragged him along with the rest of the racing crowd, trampling others beneath their feet. Children sobbed and men cried out.

Less than five minutes later, police paused to catch their breath, and some pulled cigarettes from their inside pockets. The speakers they'd apprehended had been marched off, and there was nobody left to chase. On the street, knots of breathless trekkers paused to catch their breath, too, then began to advance. Picking up stones, Joe and Pete joined the dozens dashing back into the square in a spirited counterattack that took the police by surprise. A constable stumbled, and trekkers surrounded him in seconds. Joe elbowed others aside, getting his kicks in with the rest. Pete stood gawking as white smoke puffed up overhead. Joe shoved him along as the police chased trekkers headed north and south.

Chests heaving, Joe and Pete had no idea which way they were running. They were simply relieved to be beyond the reach of clubs. Seconds later came a cry, "Here they come again. Run for it, boys!" Mounties dashed up the street, batons raised. "Look out!" Up ahead were RCMP on horseback, shouldering long leather truncheons and moving forward at a trot, the horses' iron-shod hooves clattering on the asphalt. The spectators who crowded the sidewalks found it exciting until they became part of the "fun" too. Horses mounted the sidewalks, and their riders' truncheons connected with onlookers' shoulders and skulls.

Hacking and sputtering from tear gas, Pete and Joe joined others hunkered down in alleys, too breathless to speak, listening to windows shatter. Once recovered, they dashed this way and that, watching for cops, hoping to take them by surprise. It was a crazy, potentially lethal game of tag, with downtown Regina as the playground. Within minutes, the two farm boys and other shouting trekkers discovered that they were "it." They had the Mounties on the run.

A jeering mob had forced the almighty Mounties back

to their three-storey station. Nobody had to look over their shoulder for cops now; they were lined up ahead in a neat little row. Objects of every size and description flew through the air; Mounties winced and turned away, but it was too late for some. Joe laughed as his chunk of jagged concrete found its mark and a constable fell to his knees, blood streaming down his face. Then the police began hurling tear-gas canisters. Trekkers dodged the tumbling containers, scooped them up and tossed them back. But what was this? "Watch it—that one's loadin' his gun!" A police officer was pointing his revolver over their heads. *Crack!*

The trekkers glanced at each other. Jeez! Now they're shooting at us! Screaming and yelling, they threw everything they could lay their hands on. *Crack!* The trekkers ducked instinctively at the revolver's report. *Crack-crack-crack-crack!*

As they rounded a corner, Pete, Joe and the rest practically collided with another group on the run from a mounted unit. Leaders went to work, barking orders, pushing men this way and that. The men didn't hesitate. Within seconds, 150 men, many wiping blood from their faces, began their march to the safety of the stadium. Marsh and his concertina weren't around, but just one or two voices were all it took to start the song. Then other voices picked it up:

See our numbers still increasing;
Hear the bugle blow.

By our union we shall triumph
Over every foe.

Hold the fort for we are coming.

Voices faltered and bodies collided as confusion turned to shock. Ahead, rows of Mounties on horseback were positioned across the street. "Hold!" someone bawled out. Was it Walsh, or Brodie? Joe couldn't tell. Men broke ranks, stooped down and snatched up rocks. "Here they come!" the voice shouted needlessly. Every wide-eyed man could see for himself the wall of glistening horseflesh moving relentlessly toward them.

Frantically, Joe, Pete and dozens of others raced back and began to shove parked cars into the middle of the intersection. Metal screeched and glass tinkled as eager arms tipped vehicles over. During those borrowed seconds, the other trekkers sprinted behind the barricade of old Fords, Chevs and Plymouths stretched diagonally across the broad street. Then came raucous laughter. Pedalling furiously, grinning schoolkids wheeled their bikes up behind the wall of cars. Inside their carriers and handlebar baskets were rocks, concrete and brick. The men filled their hands and pockets and piled the rest within easy reach. As the last kids pedalled away, men glimpsed the horsemen trotting toward their barricade.

"Come on, you yellow-legged sons of bitches," someone shouted. Seconds crawled past. "Now!" came the cry, and the missiles flew. The advancing Mounties yanked their reins back savagely. The horses whinnied in protest, and the cowering riders hunched down and then cantered away into the safety of a nearby alley. Behind the cars, there were triumphant shouts and screamed catcalls. Then, breathing hard, the men hunkered down. Pete closed his eyes and leaned back against a fender. He'd never been so tired. When he opened his eyes, there was Joe, sitting on a running board. Pushing his hair back from his face with a shaky hand, Joe grinned maniacally at the pavement at his feet. He likes this, Pete thought. All Pete wanted to do was curl up and go to sleep— forever. Before the night ended, fate almost granted his wish.

At the sharp sound of hooves striking the pavement, the men's heads snapped around. The Mounties had circled round, and dozens of them were galloping forward in a full-bore charge. They would be on top of the boys in seconds. Rocks flew, but the trekkers were already falling back, dodging horses and clubs. It was a rout, every man for himself.

In the hours that followed, the small knots of trekkers running and fighting on the dimly lit streets realized that the horse cops wouldn't let them reach the safety of the stadium. Joe yanked Pete into a darkened laneway, and they collapsed beside garbage cans. There was sporadic gunfire as cops on foot hunted down the trekkers. They were out for blood. Moments later, Joe shook Pete awake and pointed at a huge mob milling about three stalled streetcars in the distant intersection. Joe and Pete joined other trekkers dashing in that direction.

Inside the crowd, Pete watched a trekker scramble up onto the roof of the middle streetcar and stare down the street, past the alley he and Joe had just fled. The trekker turned, waving his arms frantically. A ripple of emotion— part fear, part excitement—ran through the crowd. City cops, in fours, strode up the sidewalk, batons swinging before the scrambling pedestrians. Behind the trolleys, trekkers hurled debris, but the police were out of range. Much of the mob shifted to the corner diagonally across from the advancing police. The cops were all bunched up, making a wonderful target. The barrage began, and cops cowered beneath the storm. One of them shouted something. Under the deadly hail, the police begin to fan out. The trekkers watched in disbelief as some cops pulled out their guns. Naw, they wouldn't . . .

Crack-crack-crack!

A man standing nearby—Joe was willing to bet he was no trekker—gasped and fell to the sidewalk. Somewhere close by a woman screamed. Pete instinctively hunched his shoulders and turned away.

Crack-crack!

Another man grunted and clutched his elbow. Joe hit the pavement and looked about. A wounded trekker, leg dragging, inched his way painfully along the tracks as he sought cover under a nearby streetcar. The air was filled with shouts, cries of pain and the slap-slap-slap of hundreds of shoes hitting the pavement as people scurried for cover.

Pete was on the ground beside Joe, screaming at him to get away. Joe nodded, and they lifted themselves into a crouch.

Crack!

Behind them, a man with "Vancouver to Ottawa" chalked on the back of his jacket moaned and slouched against the stone wall of the Bank of Nova Scotia, clutching his stomach. Two other trekkers ran to his aid. One turned and waved in Joe and Pete's direction. It was plain what he wanted. Pete backed away, allowing Joe to drag him along. Joe was right. They had no time for strangers; they had to help themselves. Even if it took all night, somehow they would sneak through the cops and find their way back to the stadium. Then, they would get out of this city. Dull, boring Arran had never seemed so appealing.

Indian Summer

Mid-September signalled the end of Banff's 1935 tourist season. It had been a good summer with no trouble to speak of. They had built a new fence around the golf course to keep elk off the newly seeded fairways. During Indian Days, Norman Luxton was made honourary chief of the Stoneys, the people he loved so much.

Gray Campbell would miss the Banff Springs Concert Trio's evening musicales—big-city culture in a small mountain village. In town, businesses were shut tight, their owners bound for sunnier climes. The Brewsters' Mount Royal Hotel managed to fill rooms, perhaps providing enough revenue to keep the hotel doors open until next season. In this stubborn economic depression, nothing was certain.

The fall and winter months stretched ahead with weeks of nothing much of anything, except the brief winter carnival. Visitors would be too cold to get into much mischief. There would be no fires to fight or poachers to reprimand, so all would be quiet for Bill Neish and other game wardens. The summer's troublesome hikers and trail riders were back home wedging new snapshots into photo corners. In a few weeks, Bill and the others would be cinching up snowshoes instead of saddling horses. The only people they were likely to meet on the trail were hardy local skiers.

At the detachment, Gray and the others welcomed new and returning men. The month before, Sergeant Tommy Wallace and his wife, Helen, had arrived from Lethbridge. On the western front, the former Sixth Gordon Highlander corporal had won the Military Medal as acting sergeant of snipers. No wonder Tommy was one of the force's best marksmen! Gray had struck up a particularly close relationship with barracks roommate Constable George "Scotty" Harrison, back from brief duty in BC. Harrison had some pretty fast moves on the soccer pitch—name a position, he played it well—and obviously he had some nice moves off the pitch too. He'd announced his engagement to brown-eyed Edith Wellman, passing the wedding ring around the barracks. The guys agreed it was a dandy.

Constable George "Nipper" Combe had transferred in

from Calgary, sharing the hair-raising saga of Drumheller's cop-killing farmer. Calgary dog man Jack Cawsey had been there, too, Nipper told them, but without his dog. It was nice for Jack, and the force, that Dale finally got an opportunity to strut his stuff. Thirty miles from Calgary, two-and-a-half-year-old Eileen Simpson had gone missing from the family farm without shoes, coat or even underwear. By dusk, after 200 searchers had given up, Cawsey got a call. The next morning, the dog and men headed out to find Eileen, who was presumed dead by this time. Trusty Dale! When the men caught up with him, he was licking the face of the semi-conscious girl. The rescue made the papers, coast-to-coast.

August had brought the provincial election victory of "Bible Bill" Aberhart and his new Social Credit Party. Voters gave the evangelist a landslide 56 seats out of 63, with John Brownlee's United Farmers of Alberta losing every single seat. The summer had started with glad tidings from Regina, at least from the perspective of the RCMP. Mounties and city police had quelled a full-scale riot. Dozens of trekkers were put firmly in their place—inside city jail cells. Too bad it cost a city detective's life to do it. He had been clubbed to death on the market square.

Nothing this exciting would ever happen in Banff. There was no chance the Mounties in this little town would face the kind of danger officers had faced in Estevan, Regina, or that Gray had faced in Edmonton. There was no chance he would ever draw his revolver. No chance whatsoever.

9

Robbery and Murder

IT WAS 11 P.M., BUT LIGHTS inside Fawcett and Smith General Store in the border hamlet of Benito, Manitoba, still beckoned late-night shoppers. Come fall, the store's partners knew it wasn't unusual for trucks or wagons to pull up this late. Those farmers who had a harvest were in the fields until dark. It might be close to 10 p.m. by the time they returned home, unhitched their teams and ate. This week, Bill Smith was taking the night shift. Ernie Fawcett would stop by around midnight. The two would count and bag the cash, flick the lights off and lock up.

Flying Cans
Behind the counter, bespectacled Fawcett heard the door

open and looked over. His jaw dropped. Three tall, slim men stood just inside the doorway, tightly tied cloths concealing their lower faces. As he stepped toward the counter, one of them pulled a small revolver from his jacket pocket, a move straight out of a Warner Brothers gangster movie.

The kid with the gun—despite the masks, it was obvious these guys were young—wrapped his left hand around Bill's neck, yanked him across the counter and jammed the gun into his chest. "Come across!" he barked. Bill raised his hands up in a gesture of surrender, but snatched one of the bottles resting on the counter. He brought the bottle across his attacker's face. The enraged kid retaliated, laying the side of his pistol smartly against Bill's ear. Bill gasped, and the bottle clanked harmlessly to the floor.

All heads turned at a shout from the rear of the store. Ernie Smith strode toward the kid, his hands grabbing cans of peas and beans lining the shelves. Close behind, Ernie's son Oscar followed. The two flung cans at the gunman, who ducked and stepped back toward his pals, jerking the gun this way and that, as if he couldn't decide who to shoot first.

As he waved the gun around, Joe was stunned. Three guys? On previous nights, they'd seen the old one in glasses, but they hadn't planned on tangling with three. Cans bounced off the wall behind him and rolled noisily across the wood floor. The old guy was rounding the near end of the counter, and the mean-looking guys in the aisle were moving closer. Three men—defiant men—definitely weren't in the plans! Stumbling into each other as they retreated, Pete and John had obviously come to the same conclusion.

"They're getting away!" Oscar raced toward the one clutching the revolver. The gun smacked down hard on the side of Oscar's head, and he reeled away. Joe pushed Pete and John through the doorway, just as a farmer stepped up from the sidewalk. Pete gave him a shove and he went sprawling.

Across town, 55-year-old William Wainwright was nodding off in his living-room chair. After dinner that night, Bill had strapped his .38 special beneath his coat and waved Eunice goodbye, off on his nightly rounds as part-time town constable. Business at the garage wasn't what it used to be, so the provincial government stipend was welcome. When Bill got back, Eunice had tea waiting. Now, their cups were empty and the teapot cold. Bill glanced up at the clock on the mantle. It was 11:15 and time to call it a night. But then the telephone jangled. Bill Wainwright's night was not quite over yet.

The meeting at the store was brief but emotional, which was no surprise to Wainwright, given the ordeal the three men had endured. Lobbing tin cans at a guy with gun? They were damn lucky to be alive, he thought. Nobody could identify the would-be robbers. Wainwright took down the details and called the RCMP detachment at Swan River, 25 miles northeast. Dauphin constable John Shaw, filling in for someone on leave, answered and said he would meet Bill the next day.

Shaw pulled a couple of young guys in for questioning, but it was only a gesture. The case was as cold as a January icicle hanging on a prairie farmhouse. The town constable had some intriguing information, though. On a couple of occasions, people recalled seeing a slightly unusual automobile—an open touring car—parked near Bill and Ernie's store.

A Fight for Freedom

Across the border in Saskatchewan, the three boys laid low for a few days. They heard and saw nothing. When they got together next, they rehashed the botched holdup. John couldn't figure Joe out. "Why didn't you shoot?" he asked.

Joe pointed at John and Pete, "And where were you two? Why didn't you rush 'em?" Their anger quickly spent, the three slouched about morosely. Threshing-crew pay was lousy. Money was tight, especially after they had shelled out cash for new suits. There were dances, too, but they cost money, as did the hooch sold outside. They'd have to do something.

Returning home from Regina had been easier than Pete and Joe had expected. The Saskatchewan government had wanted the now-disbanded trekkers to leave town as badly as the two boys did, so it gave about 1,300 trekkers train tickets to head home or go to a relief camp. It was an easy decision for the pair from Arran. No sitting up on a box-car catwalk either; they rolled east on comfy coach seats. Back home, life was as boring and frustrating as usual until they got together with John. Too bad the holdup hadn't gone right, but they'd do better next time. They had what it took to do it: Joe's little revolver (he'd never said where he got it, just that he'd learned a lot in jail) and Pete's hunting knife. Joe was still "test driving" the old touring car he hoped to buy from Ed Dubois, who needed cash almost as badly as they did.

The following Friday night, Bill Wainwright stepped briskly down the sidewalk on his rounds. Phillip, one of Bill's two sons, was still inside the garage, bent beneath the hood of an old rustbucket someone was praying he could fix. Keeping vehicles on the road was what kept the business going. And speaking of vehicles . . . what do you know! An open touring car rolled to a stop at the opposite curb. Bill stepped into the shadows. It was nothing as ostentatious as a Packard or Cadillac, which were all sleek lines and cowl vents. The beat-up thing was likely a Nash Advanced 8 or Ford Phaeton. And darned if it wasn't Joe Posnikoff behind the wheel with passengers Pete Woiken and John Kalmakoff. Bill had known them since they were tots. He'd call the Mounties, and they'd bring the kids in. They'd have a ready-made excuse since the car had no plates.

Constable John Shaw was in his room at Swan Lake's Vimy Hotel when he got the message to head down to Benito. Shaw shrugged out of his civvies—so much for his evening off. That was okay, though, since his duties kept his mind occupied. It was too easy to dwell on his fiancée, Jay Rzesnoski, waiting back in Dauphin. Shaw was counting the days until he was transferred back; he couldn't wait to see Jay again. Within minutes, the uniformed constable was walking over to Spence's Garage, where the detachment's new, unmarked, two-door Chevrolet was stored.

When Shaw arrived at Benito half an hour later, the boys were still sitting in the car. The two constables escorted them to Bill's garage, the closest place offering privacy. In Wainwright's office, Shaw patted the kids down for weapons and found nothing. There was a brief give-and-take as the boys offered vague mumbles in response to almost every question put to them. Neither officer was surprised. Getting anything useful out of distrustful Doukhobors was made tougher by the language barrier. It wasn't much easier with their Canadian-born kids, who had thick accents and fractured syntax. Shaw ordered Joe to see him in Swan River the next day about operating a vehicle without licence plates.

Cop Killers

After the boys left, Shaw speculated that police in Pelly might be able to tie the boys to an Arran incident, if not the attempted Benito holdup. That was convenient since the Pelly detachment had the nearest jail. Shaw and Wainwright decided to take the boys into custody and spent the night attempting to locate the now-vanished touring car. Had they understood the kids better, they would have begun their search a few minutes southeast of Arran, at the Vestna Hall parking lot. Laughing with relief, the three boys had roared off to another dance. On the way, they had persuaded two fun-loving girls, Frances and Pauline Ogloff, to come along.

The girls didn't think twice; it wasn't every day that three handsome guys in snappy suits in a swell car swept into the Ogloff farmyard.

It was after 2 a.m., and the boys were driving the sisters home. Headlamp beams washed over a lone figure scuffling along the road. He turned; it was Paul Bugera, from Arran. Joe hit the brakes. Young Paul vaulted into the back seat, and the happy bunch sped off, the boys guzzling from jugs of breath-taking, home-brewed "vodka." An hour or so later, the girls were gone and the fun was over. A Chevy overtook the touring car, stopped in the road and a Mountie waved Joe down. Paul heard the other three muttering ominously.

At first, Bugera was confused, but he soon got the picture: these two cops were hauling his friends in, and it wasn't just for drunk driving. Paul's confusion turned to anxiety when the uniformed cop ordered him to drive the touring car. Any other time, he would have loved to get behind the wheel of this old beaut, but now he wished he had never set eyes on it. Sometime after 5 a.m., just east of Arran, Paul's inebriation and fatigue won out over anxiety, and he drove the car into a ditch. Frustrated, Shaw shoved Paul into the back of the police car with his glowering friends and got back behind the wheel. A few minutes later, Paul Bugera was standing on the road not far from his home and watched the car disappear west toward Pelly.

Sitting directly behind Shaw, Joe Posnikoff thought quickly. The .38 in his pocket and the attempted robbery meant just one thing: jail time. He vowed he'd never go behind bars again. Next to Joe, John was turning over that two-year-old double murder. Worst luck: the fire that should have consumed the Zurawells and their house had done nothing more than singe the bedclothes. The police found bodies, bullet holes and, it was reported, fingerprints. If the cops printed him in Pelly, John was a goner. And right now, Pelly was just a few minutes away.

John nudged Pete into wakefulness. Despite those cops stumbling across them, Joe figured they still had a little luck going. Nobody had bothered to search them a second time. He had his gun, and Pete had his knife. The trouble was they might lose control of the car. Then, Shaw slowed to make the curve in the road. Joe pulled his gun, and John nudged Pete, who pulled the knife sheathed on his right hip. Raising it high, he buried the blade deep into Wainwright's hair. The Benito constable screamed in agony.

In a vain attempt to stop Pete's attack, Shaw reached back. Pete extracted the knife from Wainwright's skull and stabbed the Mountie's hand. Shaw's cry of pain mingled with Wainwright's moans. Encircling Shaw's neck with his left arm, Pete drove his knife deep into the policeman's cheek. Through his pain, Wainwright felt John's hand beneath his coat, tugging at his left side. John yanked hard and sat back, clutching Wainwright's .38. Hand still clamped to his bleeding head, Wainwright twisted about. John levelled the revolver and squeezed the trigger. A blast deafened them all, a brilliant flash illuminated the car's dark interior, and Bill Wainwright's right eye disappeared. Pete loosened his grip around Shaw as Joe pressed the muzzle of his little .32 against the Mountie's head. There were three rapid pops; blood spattered the roof fabric and the driver's doorpost. The slugs' impact threw Shaw against the steering wheel. The car slewed left, bounced off a boulder, lurched diagonally across the road and slid into the ditch.

The angle of the two-door car, not to mention the bodies slouched in front, made it tough to get out. Pushing and yanking, John managed to open the driver's door. He pulled Shaw out and dumped him on the shoulder. Pete and John climbed out and then pulled Wainwright's body free. John pointed to a clump of spruce. Within a few minutes, Shaw and Wainwright had disappeared, and the unmarked police car was parked neatly on the shoulder, the damage limited to a crumpled right rear fender and running board.

The three were elated at what the dead men's pockets revealed: over 80 dollars from the Mountie and close to 50 from the Benito cop. Then, tipsy Pete proposed a lark so crazy that John and Joe both had to stifle laughter. The effect of a mash of potatoes, sugar and yeast on Pete was amazing. In a minute or two, bloodied John Shaw lay in the mud in his underwear and socks, and behold: RCMP constable Pete Woiken, accompanied by plainclothes detectives John Kalmakoff and Joseph Posnikoff. A drunken lark had become a cunning deception. Among the simple farm folk, it was the key to a clean getaway.

10

Headed for Paradise

LATE SATURDAY MORNING, THE farm-boy killers awoke in the stolen police car, suffering pounding heads, dry mouths and rumbling stomachs. Time would cure their headaches, but only food and drink would cure the rest. They had the money to treat themselves to a great lunch, but they couldn't do it in Arran, Benito or Pelly. Pete's Mountie disguise wouldn't fool anybody. They decided to head for an isolated farm to minimize the risk and eat for free.

Lunch at Perepeluk's

The three boys weren't the only ones who awoke bleary-eyed on that October 5 morning. The day before, Bill Perepeluk had had his crew out threshing until dark, but weariness was a small price to pay for getting a crop in. The crop money wouldn't be in his pocket too long. It belonged to Canada Mortgage Corporation (CMC). Sure, Bill had got that second farm for a rock-bottom price, but the Perepeluks still owed CMC.

In the kitchen, little Ludwig was crawling happily about, and Bill's wife, Mary, was busy at the stove. Nodding to Mary's younger cousin, Bessie Chornook, Bill scooped up the infant and sat down at the table. The dog was kicking up a racket outside. Bill peeked through the curtains and saw a car slowing down. Bill knew few people who owned a car, and nobody owned a new one. Who could it be? He sighed. The guy from CMC, that's who.

"Who the hell let him know to come so quick?" Bill asked Mary. "I no sooner get threshed and he wants to know how many bushels."

Bill's jaw dropped when he saw three men emerge from the car. "I'll be damned; it's cops!" He handed the baby to Bessie and made for the door.

The dog was going berserk, ignoring Bill's calls. The smiling men moved toward the porch, and Bill noticed the dog was interested in the car, not the men. The mutt was on his hind legs, sniffing around the door windows—strange. With barely a smile and nod in his direction, the uniformed one marched right past Bill and into the kitchen, followed by the two in suits. Arrogant sons-of-guns! Bill meekly stepped in and shut the door.

Mary was Missus Hospitality and typically curious, asking, "What are you doing way out here?" For farmers' wives living "way out here," unexpected guests were a welcome novelty.

"We're looking for a couple of guys," Joe said.

"Trouble at the Vestna dance last night," John put in quickly.

"Oh," Bill chuckled, taking Ludwig back from Bessie. "Who got the black eye?"

"Oh, no, no," Pete smiled, "We're looking for the guys that robbed the Fawcett and Smith store in Benito and killed Wainwright and a policeman." John shot Joe a quick glance. Damn! Why had Pete told them all that?

Bill and Mary stared at each other, open-mouthed. Bill Wainwright was dead? Poor Eunice! They had heard about the attempted store robbery—despite the rural isolation, news got around—but murders? Why hadn't they heard about this?

Before Bill could ask, one of the guys in a suit blurted out that the three were searching for the killers. Then, nodding toward the steaming pots on the stove, he asked if they could have lunch. Bill sat down and bounced Ludwig on his knee to mask his irritation at the men, bold as brass, asking for lunch without waiting for the invitation. He shot Mary an inquiring look, but his wife's attention was on one of the men.

"Aren't you Joe Posnikoff?" she asked lightly.

Joe's smile stuck on his face, and he cursed inwardly.

He knew he recognized her from somewhere. Arran's two-storey school, that's where. She was Mary Keneschuk, the one in braids. There was no help for it now; he'd have to bluff it out. He nodded at Pete and John, whose smiles were as wooden as his, and introduced them.

"I didn't know you were a cop," Mary said to Joe.

"Oh, after I went to school, I went away to be a cop," Joe shrugged. "I'm just helping out here."

After an easygoing lunch, Joe coaxed Perepeluk outside to "have a look around." It was soon obvious to Bill it was merely an excuse to get him out of the house. The policemen wanted his assurances that he wouldn't tell anybody about their visit. Secrecy, it seemed, was a must. Suddenly, Mountie Woiken was backing out from behind the Chevy's passenger seat, holding a half-gallon jug. Bill liked a drink as much as the next man, but not with policemen, who usually busted up stills as soon as they found them. Nevertheless, the nervous farmer clinked glasses with his guests. Then, the fun really began.

John and Joe liked this "cousin Bessie." She hadn't yet turned into a dowdy farmer's wife with a squalling kid on her hip. "Wanna see our handcuffs?" John said, as he motioned to Pete to hand them over. Suddenly Pete seemed awfully quiet. Maybe it was the booze. Sullenly, he extended the bracelets to John. "Do you wanna feel 'em?" John asked Bessie. He clicked the cuffs around Bessie's wrists.

Despite his empty glass, Bill Perepeluk was as sober as the day he was born. This was crazy. No policeman would act this way. "Wanna see my gun?" Abruptly, John reached beneath his suit coat and whipped out a revolver. Then, Mountie Pete pulled a hunting knife. Did Mounties carry knives? Handcuffed Bessie, smiling nervously, extended her wrists, wanting out. Woikin staggered to his feet, fumbling with a key ring. It was obvious he couldn't find the right key. Was it because he was drunk or because he didn't know which key to use? There was relieved laughter when the cuffs sprang open and Bessie yanked free. A few minutes later, the police were shouting goodbye, and the Chevy bounced out of the yard. Fifty years later, Bill Perepeluk would still recall this visit with crystal clarity, thankful they were all still alive at the end of it.

A few miles down the dusty road, the shouting began. Joe had led them straight to a girl he had known from school! Fuming behind the wheel, Pete darted a glance at Joe in the rear-view mirror and gave him a piece of his mind.

Joe pushed Pete's shoulder. Pete had told Perepeluk and his wife too much. Pete missed the curve and hit the ditch. Struggling out of the car, the boys were in an ugly mood, but hid it quickly as a passing farmer stopped to offer help. Together, the four managed to right the car.

After abortive attempts to see relatives, who weren't at home, the three decided it was no good killing police-men if you couldn't boast about it. So, later that day, at the farm of John Legebokoff, they stunned the farmer by lifting a blanket to reveal the bloodstained front seats. They had to be fooling! Legebokoff thought, but as they waved their guns around, he wasn't so sure. The one in uniform asked Legebokoff's frightened daughter to come for a spin, but she declined. He was hesitating about going along with the others, who then started threatening him and pushing him around. Damned if he didn't start crying! Like Bill Perepeluk, Legebokoff would never forget that bizarre visit.

Later, the boys showed up at an afternoon wedding reception and took in a dance at Stenberg's converted granary that night. However, they knew they couldn't hang around. The search would be on for the missing cops. But where would they go? As they drove aimlessly through southeast Saskatchewan, they came up with the answer: the Kootenays. British Columbia.

The Kootenay Doukhobor colonies operated sawmills, thousands of acres of fruit orchards and a huge factory at Brilliant that produced famous jams that sold by the boxcar clear across Canada. Compared to Saskatchewan, the place was paradise. When they told those Doukhobors their names, in Russian, the boys were convinced they would be taken in and given food, jobs and money. The Mounties would never find them. The three headed west.

The Stolen Car

On Monday afternoon, October 7, radio station CFAC got a telephone call from the RCMP's town station, requesting it to air a bulletin on a stolen police car that carried Manitoba plates. Delighted the police needed its help, CFAC broadcast the bulletin. Radio was fine for music, *Amos 'n' Andy* and *The Shadow*, but it was regarded as the bastard child of the press, the legitimate news source. CFAC boys wouldn't have been nearly so pleased if they'd known the RCMP contacted American stations too.

A few hours earlier, inside the two-storey, highway-fronting home of Bob Straw and his family, 15 miles east of Banff, Margaret and daughter Lillian had been at work in the little living-room cafe. Good weather and road crews had kept the restaurant and gas pumps open beyond the summer season. Through the curtains, Lillian watched three young fellows in rumpled suits pile out of a Chevrolet that looked as travel worn as they did. Lillian didn't like what she saw. They were shady-looking characters with caps pulled low over their eyes.

"There are some fellows out there who look like they could kill someone," Lillian told her mother.

"Well, if you feel that way, just give them what they want," Margaret said. What Lillian felt like doing was turning the Open sign to Closed, but it was too late; the three were already inside.

"Roast beef sandwiches and coffee is all that's left," Lillian said, forcing a smile. She poured the coffee, but couldn't get up the nerve to make conversation. The song on the radio, a catchy but dumb little ditty called "You're Nothin' but a Nothin'" was an irritating intrusion. Lillian snapped it off.

"Get it back on," mumbled one of the three into the silence. Lillian snapped on the music again.

After eating, the three rose to leave, but some of the thirsty road crew appeared, eager to buy pop. The three sat back down and didn't move until the crewmen left. Lillian thought she understood. They were having difficulty coming up with the money to pay. After some scrounging about, they managed the 45 cents required. Through the window, Lillian could see them standing by the car, obviously trying to decide which way to go. When the car sped away, she reached for the phone.

No, Canmore RCMP constable Jack Bonner told Lillian patiently, he couldn't arrest them just because she had suspicions. Lillian stammered a thank you and hung up, feeling foolish.

Inside the Chevrolet, the weary prairie boys were on edge. The late afternoon was chilly, and they had no coats or gloves. The nearby mountains loomed alien and forbidding in the growing twilight. Their money was almost gone, spent on gas, good times and the two rifles they had added to their arsenal. The Chevy's gas was low. A sign pointed to Exshaw. Joe wheeled off the highway, and they saw the lights burning brightly at Roy Zeller's garage. The boys bought a gallon of gas and drove off. The red tail lights were still glimmering in the distance when Roy's wife, Lucille, dashed up breathlessly from their house next door. "That's a stolen police car. It's on that Seattle radio station!" she yelled. Roy ran home and shouted at the long-distance operator to put him through to Canmore RCMP.

Inside the white wood-frame house that served as both family residence and RCMP office and jail, Jack Bonner stared at the telephone. The licence number confirmed it was a stolen police car. Roy described the three young guys, likely the same ones who had scared Lillian Straw.

Jack moved quickly. He hollered at his teenage son to run down the road to Bob Hawke's place and tell the part-time police magistrate to get armed and be ready for pickup. Jack knew the war vet could handle himself. Chained to a desk as Canmore Mines payroll clerk, Bob would likely relish the diversion. It was only a stolen car, but he'd amuse the others at the office with the tale. Bonner's next call was to the Banff detachment.

Gray Campbell, the telephone orderly that night, answered. He listened as Jack Bonner related particulars of the Zeller call. "She heard it on a radio broadcast?" the dubious Gray wondered aloud. "We've had no word from Calgary or Edmonton." A fine state of affairs, he thought to himself, when the public knew more than they did. "They couldn't get *this* far without our knowing."

Jack Bonner had no time to debate the finer points of communications protocol with a younger, by-the-book rookie. "Could be a stolen car headed your way," he insisted. Unable to pull rank on another constable, Jack decided to put Gray to work. "So, what'll we do?" he asked.

"You better not stop it alone," Gray answered firmly. "We'll drive down to meet you."

Attaboy! "Look for Manitoba plates," Bonner barked, "Three men."

Nipper Combe turned up in civvies, ready for a night off. Gray asked him to call Scotty back from his patrol a few streets away and got Constable Jim Eaton to man the phones. Gray told them what he knew. They'd find off-duty Tommy Wallace and hit the highway. Nipper retrieved his revolver, and they signed out another for the sergeant.

Inside the Lux Theatre, Tommy and his wife were watching *Dante's Inferno* and its Hollywood-style Hades. He met Nipper and Scotty in the lobby, then ducked back into the theatre to tell Helen he was off, leaving her to see what would happen to Spencer Tracy and Claire Trevor. Gray Campbell steered the Terraplane down Banff Avenue, unknowingly driving the four of them straight to a hell of their own.

11

The End of the Road

THE SASKATCHEWAN BOYS WERE humiliated. A two-dollar fee to simply drive through Banff park? Denied entry at the little gatehouse, the near-penniless trio headed east again, but only for a few miles. They'd had enough of being broke. Joe made a U-turn and pulled over to the shoulder. There, they waited impatiently for their next victim. Within moments, headlights appeared in the rear-view mirror. Flashlight in hand, Joe jumped out, but he was too late to wave down the car roaring by in a blinding cloud of dust.

Inside the speeding car, Jack Bonner and Bob Hawke exchanged glances. Was that the car? That guy stepping out—was that a gun in his hand? A few hundred yards west, the pair decided to check. Bonner killed the engine, cut the lights and, revolvers drawn, the constable and the part-time magistrate took to the bush.

The Traveller and his Wife

Just over 13 miles east of Banff, Calgary-based commercial traveller C. Thomas Scott and his wife were heading into the mountains for a quiet, off-season getaway. Scott had earned the respite. Life for a door-to-door salesman peddling everything from cleaning products to spices and ointments wasn't an easy one. However, the Rawleigh products he sold enjoyed a good reputation, and likeable Scott was as much a family friend as a persuasive salesman. He was doing okay.

Scott slowed as he saw a light ahead. A young man holding a flashlight stood with two others next to a parked car. Although they looked respectable—they wore suits—you couldn't be too careful these days. Scott extracted their $85 of holiday money from his coat pocket and deftly wedged the bills between the seat cushion and the back of the seat.

"We're out of gas," Joe Posnikoff told Scott through his open window. Mrs. Scott turned; a second man stood outside her window.

"I'll be glad to give you some, if you've got a container of some sort," the affable Scott replied. Without warning, he found himself staring at a drawn gun. John Kalmakoff levelled a revolver at his wife.

Joe yanked Scott's door open. "Get out and hold your hands

The End of the Road

RCMP constables Campbell (left) and Combe in a photograph belatedly published in the *Calgary Albertan*. GRAY CAMPBELL FONDS, UNIVERSITY OF VICTORIA LIBRARIES SPECIAL COLLECTIONS

high," he ordered. Standing on the road, Scott was relieved of $10 in change. "Is that all you have?" Joe asked incredulously. "Sure there's no more in the car?"

Scott had worked damned hard for that hidden roll of bills. "There's no more," he said firmly.

"If there is, you know what it means," Joe warned. Scott wasn't exactly sure *what* it meant, but decided to hold his tongue and take his chances.

"Is there money in that purse, Madame?" John asked the woman sitting in the passenger seat.

"Yes," came the hesitant reply.

Scott shrugged and smiled sheepishly. His wife thrust her purse at John through her open window. "When you're being held up, you can't think of everything!" she said defiantly. Joe glanced over. The old biddy had guts! John stepped away and took the measure of the man standing calmly before him, pockets turned inside out, arms raised. The gun hadn't rattled him.

Bonner and Hawke crouched in the bush just above the highway. All they could make out were the dim outlines of two cars and a group of people. To make it worse, the second car's headlights had inexplicably snapped off moments after the car came to a halt, plunging the whole scene into the gloom. They were too far away to hear what was being said. The two lawmen didn't have a clue what was going on.

John Kalmakoff tossed the purse back to the woman. There were just a few bucks, but it was better than nothing. He opened the door, ushered her out and prodded her around the car. Pete walked up and motioned his pals over.

Talk flew back and forth. What now? They had got all the money they were likely to get. How soon would it be before the police caught up with them? Was that why the guy at the gate wanted all that information about the car? Maybe they should switch cars.

Scott couldn't understand the foreign language the men spoke, but he heard the word "police" a couple of times. Watching them, huddled together, waving their guns around, their breath clouding the cold night air, the salesman started to put it together. These three were making this up as they went along.

One of them walked over to the Scotts' car and got behind the wheel. Great, Scott thought. Now they're gonna steal our car. For some reason, the kid couldn't get the engine to turn over. He got out, slamming the door in disgust.

Joe walked back to the couple. Scott listened in disbelief as the gunman told them he and his friends had to get across the border to BC. Scott's customers, some of them sad and lonely, confided all kinds of crazy things, but a guy who's just robbed you, sharing his gang's plans? It was bizarre.

The three huddled again, and this time spoke in heavily accented English. What should they do about these two? They would talk to police. Do we kill them? The Scotts stared at each other in horror. A simple robbery was turning into a life-and-death affair. After surviving Passchendaele and Vimy Ridge as a Princess Pat, what a cruel joke it would be if he was shot down in peaceable

Canada by some foreign punk! Scott lowered his hands. Joe stepped up, jerking the gun at him. Scott raised his hands higher and watched the robber's eyes travel up to his wristwatch. "Take it," Scott offered.

Joe slid the watch off and examined it. He told Scott he didn't really want it; it was money they needed, but he was willing to make a deal. "If you don't tell the police, I'll return your watch."

Nonplussed, Scott nodded, wondering if this could get any crazier, and Joe handed him back his watch. "Now!" he shouted, "Get in your car and drive like the dickens! We'll follow right behind, and if you tell the police, we will kill you and the police will kill us."

The Scotts scrambled into their car, which, thankfully, started without any trouble. They watched the boys get into their Chevy up ahead. "And the police will kill us." The words replayed in Scott's head. It was pure fatalism, like Bonnie and Clyde. Nonetheless, he felt relieved. They were safer now than they'd been since they were stopped. Scott put the car in gear and rolled onto the road, while Bonner and Hawke stumbled unnoticed toward their parked car.

Highway Shootout

Less than a mile west, two young constables sat in the back seat of the Terraplane, speculating heatedly about what they had learned at the gatehouse. Sitting next to Gray, Sergeant Tommy Wallace dug him in the side, biting down on his laughter. Gray understood why. It was just a stolen car. The former First World War sniper possessed a sardonic, self-deprecating sense of humour. During patrols, Tommy had walked fearlessly onto roads, arm raised, to stop suspicious cars. "Aren't you at risk?" a friend, Reverend E.R. Brundage, once had asked.

"Yes I am," Tommy had answered nonchalantly. "We all take risks. They have the drop on us and if I get mine, it's just too bad for me!" Gray had heard it tonight at the gates. Smiling, Tommy's parting comment to the gatekeepers was, "We'll see you as we come back, if we're still alive."

The fast-moving car began to slew. Road construction had reduced the surface to a dusty powder. The haze was pierced by two sets of oncoming headlights. "Should we stop them?" Gray asked.

"I think so," Tommy said, his smile gone.

Gray turned the wheel. "I'll angle across the road so they can't sneak by." Tommy nodded. As the car came to a halt, the sergeant opened his door and stepped out. Gray pulled at the door handle and felt a hand squeeze his shoulder.

"Stay where you are, laddie," Scotty mumbled in his ear. "You're the driver." Scotty squeezed past the folded-back passenger seat. Nipper Combe and Gray Campbell peered through the windshield as the two men walked toward the first approaching car.

Thank God—a police uniform! Scott leaned out of the car door and shouted, "Bandits! In the car behind us!" The policeman in civvies glanced at Scott's licence plate, then waved him on, while the other motioned the police car to back up. Scott slammed the door and stomped on the gas. One of two officers emerging from their car waved him goodbye. Didn't they get it? As he passed, Scott shouted out again, "Bandits!"

What did he say? Gray wondered, sliding behind the wheel. He angled the vehicle back across the highway. He and Nipper got out, watching Scotty walk toward the oncoming headlights a few steps to the left of Tommy Wallace, obscured now by swirling dust.

Inside their stolen Chevrolet, the boys watched a car roll across the road ahead. Out stepped a man in uniform— Mounties! They were trapped! Watching from the back seat, Pete then saw the cops' car back away. "Now, now. Drive!" he screamed. Too late! Two cops were already walking toward them, one raising his arm in a stop command. They were so close, neither John nor Joe could miss. Up came Shaw's .45 and Wainwright's .38, their muzzles almost touching the windshield.

A gunshot sounded, then another. At the Terraplane, Gray and Nipper pulled revolvers and squinted into the swirling haze. What the heck was going on?

Three yards from the suspect's car, Scotty saw Wallace stumble. A split second later, he reeled from a burning blow just below his throat. Scotty fumbled at his holster flap, barely aware that Wallace was already shooting. Damned

Bullet holes are clearly visible in the headlights and windshield of the 1935 two-door Chevrolet police car.

WHYTE MUSEUM OF THE CANADIAN ROCKIES M192 FILE 2

headlights! Scotty fired, and the far headlight winked out. He swung his revolver, and the other headlight exploded in a tinkle of glass. Then he crumpled, his head and shoulders falling beneath the front of the car.

Shouts filled the Chevy, "Go! Go!" But the cop car was blocking the road again. The cop in civvies was still on his feet. "Run him down!" The boys ducked as Wallace shot. "Out! Out!" John yanked his door open and crouched down behind the rear fender, firing, with Pete beside him. As Joe tumbled out, he felt a bullet groove his wrist. He took a step or two and gasped as another bullet hit him in the chest.

More shots. At the Terraplane, Gray and Nipper saw headlights blink out. Who was shooting whom? A ripple of air tugged at Gray's pant leg, and he realized that someone was shooting at *him*! He jumped out of the headlight's beam. Tommy emerged from the dust, firing. He turned to Gray. "More ammo!" he demanded, left hand pressed against his chest. "I've been hit," he murmured. Gray lunged through the open right door and a moment later handed Wallace a handful of cartridges. Long seconds crawled by while Gray and Nipper kept up the gunfire. Wallace snapped his reloaded revolver shut and stepped out beyond the car. He pointed his gun and shot once before collapsing in the dust. Grasping him under the armpits, Gray dragged him to the car.

Nipper heard heavy footsteps pound past. A swiftly moving shadow angled across the highway. The bastard's getting away! he thought. Nipper darted to the rear fender and fired at the fleeing man. Had he hit him? He ran to Gray and grabbed the sergeant's feet. Together, they managed to lever Wallace into the car and onto the back seat. The panting men straightened up. Nipper pointed. Gray squinted and saw, beneath the gunmen's car, a raised arm waving a revolver. He and Nipper approached the car, guns drawn, then noticed the familiar britches stripe. Nipper eased the car back, and Gray tugged at Scotty. "I've been hit," Scotty mumbled, struggling to his feet. He clamped his hand over his lower throat. "I got mine too soon," he whispered.

A car lurched around the suspects' vehicle and slid to a halt. Bonner and Hawke jumped out. They had seen what Gray and Nipper hadn't: two men making for the bush. The constable and magistrate dashed past, firing as they went. As Gray and Nipper half-carried Scotty to their car, they heard answering shots in the distance.

Minutes later, the four lawmen huddled beside the Terraplane. Bonner and Hawke wanted to flush out the fugitives. It was best that someone in uniform drove the wounded men to the closest hospital and informed Calgary station. Moments later, with Tommy stretched out in the back, and Scotty slumped in the front, Gray Campbell drove as fast as he dared toward Canmore. The ruts and potholes of the rotten road had never mattered before, but they did now. "Go slow, it hurts," Tommy gasped. And then, "They had the drop on us, Gray. We had no chance."

Harrison's every exhalation was a liquid-sounding wheeze. Gray glanced to his right. "Is it bad, Scotty?" Scotty pointed just below his Adam's apple. Even in the gloom, Gray could see the hole, pulsing blood. "We'll soon be there. You'll be okay."

"Listen to me," Scott gurgled, staring through the windshield. "It's bad; I haven't long."

Gray didn't want to listen, but he had no choice. In a halting rasp, Scotty talked about what was most important in his life. Gray strained to catch the slurred words and heard Edith Wellman's name. "Tell her I was thinking of her."

"Save it," Gray said, biting down hard, willing his chin to remain firm, his eyes to stay clear, hands clenching the wheel to remain steady. Behind him, Tommy Wallace groaned.

Kneeling behind a fallen tree between Bonner and Hawke, Nipper Combe didn't know exactly where to shoot, and he wasn't eager to raise his head to catch the muzzle flashes. Nipper's mind was full of farmer Knox and the Rosebud standoff. Most officers never faced gunfire. What were the odds that he would face it twice within six months? Frustrated, Combe finally headed back to the cars in a crouching run. As luck would have it, the shootout had begun not 40 yards from the highway crew's camp. Anyone in the bunkhouse must have heard the shooting, but did they see anything? Yes, but what crew boss Ferdinand Goetz told him merely confirmed what Nipper had already guessed: the two they'd pinned down were Scott's would-be robbers.

Gray Campbell returned a few minutes later (the men were in hospital, and Calgary was sending reinforcements), to find the two gunmen had escaped. The four lawmen decided to split up to stop traffic. Nipper had barely begun to drive west with Gray when he noticed a suspicious shape above the south shoulder. At the same moment, Gray saw headlights approaching. Both men jumped from the car, Gray running up the road to flag down the motorist, and Nipper cautiously approaching the roadside bush.

The End of the Road

Lying near the shoulder of the road, gasping in agony from his wounds, Joe Posnikoff watched the police car roll by. Any hope that it would merely disappear to the west died when the car stopped. Now one cop, his torso backlit by the headlight beams, approached. Joe extended Wainwright's revolver. So, this is it, then, the end of the road. Any moment now . . . take him with me. Then an unexpected bright light forced Joe to squeeze his eyes shut.

The beam of Nipper's flashlight revealed a man lying prone with a gun in his hand. Nipper cut his flashlight, pointed his revolver where he thought he saw the gunman and fired. Gray raced up. "I've got him!" Nipper shouted. The flashlight beam revealed a motionless man, quite dead, his arm outstretched and his hand clutching a .38.

It was close to 10 p.m. when the telephone rang in Jack Cawsey's Calgary home. A few minutes later, the sergeant was upstairs changing into his uniform, his trembling fingers fumbling with his buttons and his leave on hold. He might have waited years to test Dale's skills against armed men, but now, just six months after Rosebud, here was the opportunity. On the way to Banff, Cawsey picked up two constables—and Dale.

The next morning, Bill Neish was in Lake Louise when he got the news that two Mounties had been gunned down and the fugitives were still at large. Some wardens had already been called up, including old Walter Peyto, who had driven Tommy Wallace's wife to his hospital bedside in Calgary.

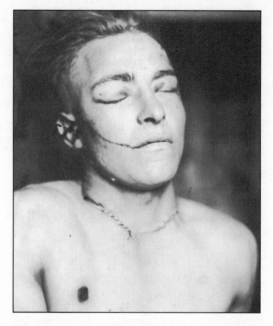

Joe Posnikoff, leader of the farm-boy trio of thieves and murderers, in a post-autopsy photograph. WHYTE MUSEUM OF THE CANADIAN ROCKIES M192 FILE 2

Neish wasn't waiting to be asked. He telephoned Banff barracks, identified himself, said he knew the country and asked if they needed his help. Within minutes, armed with his .303 rifle, Bill hitched a ride to Banff.

12

Trumpets and Empty Saddles

BY 10 A.M. TUESDAY MORNING, October 8, local volunteers and Mounties from as far away as Edmonton were poised to hunt down the two remaining fugitives. Irricana constable Richard Fenn renewed acquaintances with fellow Rosebud veterans Nipper Combe and Jack Cawsey. The latest news came from Calgary's Colonel Belcher Hospital. Sergeant Tommy Wallace was dead. Nearby, George "Scotty" Harrison still lingered, his fiancée, Edith Wellman, at his side.

Winter had arrived overnight, bringing plunging temperatures and sleet that threatened to become snow. Inside the Straws' café, which had become their field headquarters, posse members warmed up, gulped coffee and munched food. Men looked through the windows and thought of the shivering fugitives. You wouldn't want to be out in the bush too long in this stuff. Bob Hawke, the lucky stiff, wouldn't be out in the weather at all. Another kind of duty had called. He had headed out to meet the payroll train and then go back to his office. "Lucky" was not the word Hawke would have used. For the rest of his life, he would resent the fact that his job called him away on this day.

Some of the men, including Gray Campbell, George Combe and Jack Cawsey, were already cold and weary. The night before, at Cochrane, west of Calgary, Cawsey and his two constables had searched the westbound train. By midnight, with the killers' bullet-riddled car locked away in Straw's garage, Dale was sniffing around the café next door, trying to pick up the scent of Lillian's suspicious diners. ("You should have reported them to police," an incredulous Robert Hawke had admonished her. "I *did*," Lillian had huffed.) Dale had had no luck the night before, and his luck was no better that morning as he led Cawsey and others more than three miles into the bush and down the railroad tracks.

Seven Mile Hill

At the park's east gate, Gray Campbell and Bill Neish spotted each other among the milling men. Bill was anxious to get to work. "What should I do?" he asked.

"I don't know, Bill," Gray confessed. At this point, they'd split the men up into various units. "Better wait right here until someone in charge gives you a job," was the best Gray could do. But who was in charge? Inspector Arthur Birch from Banff? Or Inspector Ernie Bavin, who was expected from Calgary? Bill nodded. He understood that in crisis situations, the chain of command sometimes became convoluted.

The warden watched Gray dash away. The young man, running on adrenalin, was still on highway patrol. As soon as they were relieved, Campbell and Combe would hit their pillows, only to awaken to the awful reality of their sergeant's death. Bill remembered how tight-knit a detachment could be. Losing Wallace would hurt, and if Harrison didn't pull through . . . It was best not dwell on that. They had to find those murderous bastards, and Neish knew they wouldn't do that hanging around the east gate.

As Bill talked with parks storeman Harry Leacock, a car pulled up. A volunteer jumped out and walked over. Returning from Banff with posse rations, he and his driver had spotted two figures who looked like volunteers, two miles west, on the snow-swept highway. When they stopped to offer them coffee seconds later, the men had vanished. What now, Bill wondered. Should he still try to find someone in charge? Pardon me, sir, but there's been a report of two men on the highway just west of here. Do you think we should investigate? He'd had enough of waiting and wondering. "Drive us up there," he told the volunteer. An hour later, wet and cold, Bill and Harry emerged from the bush. They had found nothing. A truck stopped with another report: two men on the road, farther west, at Seven Mile Hill. A car pulled up and its two occupants reported their own sighting. Seconds later, with Harry standing on the left running board and Bill on the right with his rifle butt pressed against his hip, the car made a U-turn and headed toward the hill.

Shivering with cold and fatigue, John Kalmakoff and Pete Woiken looked down on the highway. If it snowed any harder, it would be all but invisible. That meant they'd be invisible, too. The snow was the first piece of luck they'd had since the night before. Once they'd eluded the police in the dark, the pointless "if only" talk had begun. If only the police hadn't arrived. If only John hadn't lost his .32. If only Pete hadn't dropped his .45. Desperate, John and Pete had sprinted back to the car to grab the rifle John now held. A rifle and a knife—that was all they had. Pete had stopped talking about looking for Joe after John told him to can it. Joe had likely been arrested or—both had heard that single gunshot—he now lay dead. They had to look out for themselves now.

Less than a mile away, Dale strained on the leash, leading Jack Cawsey and two others through the trees toward Seven Mile Hill. The dog led them on an erratic path, back and forth, up and down. Suddenly they heard gunshots ahead. They were on to the fugitives now, but who was shooting whom?

"Come out! Surrender!" Bill Neish yelled. Moments before, he and Harry had noticed tracks in the snow. They looked up and saw the two men who had made the tracks at the same instant the fugitives spotted them. A rifle came up fast—too fast, thankfully—and two shots went wide. As

Pete Woiken scrambled for cover, John Kalmakoff levered another shell into the chamber and sent a third bullet toward the lawman shouting at them from below.

"Duck!" Bill shouted to Harry, who was already on his knees, half concealed by brush. Using the trunk of a spruce to steady his aim, Bill sighted up the slope. He couldn't see anyone now, but calculated where the two were headed and fired three times in quick succession. Then Bill saw something—not much more than a smudge against the snow, but he aimed. *Crack!* A man screamed.

There was no doubt in Harry's mind. He glanced at the warden. "You got one, Bill!"

Pete collapsed to his hands and knees, head hanging. John gaped, watching him thrash in agony.

Harry glanced up the slope again. "Look out, there's another behind a log with the rifle!"

Bill peered around the tree. "Where?" Harry pointed. "Surrender! Come out with your hands up!" Bill shouted. The answer was another bullet whining down the slope. The gunman was behind that log, all right. Leacock fired his revolver in answer.

At the sound of the gunfire, Dale lurched up the slope, men clambering up behind.

"They're behind those logs!" Bill shouted over to Cawsey.

The sergeant realized immediately who was in charge here: the warden. He also realized something else. They were all directly in the line of fire. "Scatter, scatter!" he shouted.

Dale went into a frenzy. After years of training, the German shepherd's reaction to the sight of a man holding a rifle was instinctive. When Jack Cawsey's boot slipped on the snow-covered ground, the sergeant acted instinctively, too, and extended his hands to break his stumble. Sensing the loosening of the leash he had been fighting against, Dale sprang forward.

Bill Neish levelled his rifle again, aiming just slightly under the telltale barrel. *Crack!* "Ya got 'im, Bill!" Harry shouted ecstatically. But as he turned, Harry saw the snarling dog lunge for the warden.

Dale's attack took Bill Neish completely by surprise. Luckily, the dog wasn't trained to go for the throat, just a pant leg, or in this case, a coat sleeve. Still, nerves stretched taut, Bill turned the air blue, "Get this goddamn dog offa me!"

Jack Cawsey was screaming, too, "Dale! Dale!" Neish looked crazed enough to use his rifle on the dog. Cawsey wrapped his fingers around Dale's collar, yanked the dog away from Neish and pointed him up the slope. Dale took off, the men following.

When the men caught up, growling Dale had his forepaws planted on the back of one moaning fugitive, while the other writhed about nearby. Cawsey pulled the dog off and Constable Fenn turned the man over. He was lying on top of a rifle. Fenn handcuffed him. Cawsey and Dale turned to the second man. Cawsey extracted a hunting knife from the man's belt. With this much blood and muck about, it was difficult to tell how badly the men had been hit. Stomach wounds, maybe. At that moment, nobody gave it a second thought, but they soon did. How did you sustain a stomach wound lying on the ground? Maybe those two would shed some light on it, once they were hospitalized.

Aftermath

But the two boys from Saskatchewan never told anybody anything. Out cold when wheeled through the emergency doors of Banff Mineral Springs Hospital, neither regained consciousness. Pete Woiken died just after 5 p.m. that afternoon. Constable George "Scotty" Harrison succumbed to his wound just a few minutes later. Eighteen-year-old John Kalmakoff, his blood soaking a second mattress, breathed his last just past noon the following day.

In the days that followed, solemn funerals took place with all the pomp the RCMP could muster: slow-marching Mounties with reversed arms, horses with boots reversed in the stirrups, firing parties squeezing off final salutes, and trumpeters playing the mournful last post. Constable John Shaw was laid to rest in little Swan River. In Calgary, where Gray and Nipper were among Scotty's pallbearers, 8,000 spectators witnessed the sombre spectacle of a double funeral for Harrison and Wallace. Banff had wanted Harrison's funeral and finally got it, after the double funeral had served its most important purpose in Calgary. The bodies of Pete Woiken and Joe Posnikoff, unclaimed by family,

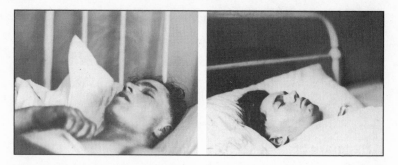

Pete Woiken (left) and John Kalmakoff (right) breathe their last in Banff Mineral Springs Hospital.

were interred near the Stoney cemetery at Morley, just east of Canmore. John Kalmakoff was buried in an unmarked grain field, a few miles southeast of Kamsack, Saskatchewan.

In Banff, questions were asked in living rooms, restaurants and on the street, and very likely inside the RCMP barracks. If the two men had been shot in the stomach, that meant they had been on their feet. Were they trying to surrender when Bill shot them? The question was never addressed at the inquests, where Neish's statements conflicted somewhat with Cawsey's. None of this surprised George "Nipper" Combe, who, along with Gray Campbell, testified at both the Calgary and Banff inquests. Once again, Nipper relived the aftermath of the Rosebud standoff. Nobody could resolve all the mysteries there, either. Neither senior officer, Birch nor Bavin, was called to testify. They had nothing to contribute.

There was another, more important question on the constables' minds. How the devil had volunteers—a game warden and a parks-stores guy, for Pete's sake!—found the fugitives when more than 30 police officers couldn't? Adding insult to injury, the shooting had started before real law-enforcement officers had arrived. By the time Cawsey and his "world-famous" dog had got there, it had been all over! There were a few snickers about Dale gnawing on Bill Neish.

But the public knew a hero when it saw one, and it wasn't a stalwart Mountie. As the *Herald*'s front-page headline made abundantly clear, it was William Neish: WARDEN SHOOTS 2 GUNMEN, THIRD DEAD. The newspaper treated Constable Nipper Combe's actions as an afterthought. It was Friday before the *Calgary Albertan* recognized the "Police Heroism" of Gray and Nipper, perhaps at the force's insistence. By then, the incident was already old news.

Bill Neish never talked publicly about the incident, shunning the limelight. Grandstanding wasn't his style, and he had to live and work alongside the Mounties. He didn't want any animosity, even though many locals thought there was some. It didn't help when the *Los Angeles Times* published a photo of Bill Neish, standing next to his horse and looking like a cowboy, under the headline FORMER MOUNTIE STILL GETS HIS MEN, without any mention of Constable Combe. The disposition of senior RCMP officers was not improved by the *Albertan*'s hasty editorial, "Someone has Blundered," which held them responsible for

Bill Neish posed willingly for this "action" shot taken after the manhunt, exchanging his game-warden uniform for Wild West cowboy garb. The photo was never published.

GLENBOW ARCHIVES NA-2778-2

the deaths of two Alberta officers through "a lack of appreciation at the essentials of criminal detection."

The day before, a *Herald* editorial, "A Warning to Authorities," had focused on the incident's wider lessons. Four dead police officers should "shock Canadian authorities into paying close attention to the immigration of people from Central European countries," the newspaper stated. "The trio of lawbreakers concerned bore the names of woykin [*sic*], Kalmakoff and Posnikoff, sufficient identification of the country from which they or their parents came originally, a country in which life is held cheap . . . their desperate last-minute defiance of law and order officers indicates the need of the most searching investigation before applicants for admission into Canada from several European countries are given permission to enter the country."

Quite soon after, RCMP vehicles became visibly identified as such and installed with radios. Trainees at Regina Depot were repeatedly reminded to search and handcuff all suspects upon apprehension. Sergeant Jack Cawsey's report concluded, "We would have overtaken them [the fugitives] as Dale was leading us right along the line they travelled." That was good enough. Less than four weeks after the shootout, the RCMP purchased Dale (K470) and quickly established Canada's first police-dog training facility near Calgary.

Epilogue

WILLIAM NEISH RETIRED AS GAME warden in 1941 and became a guard in prisoner-of-war camps in Lethbridge and Seebe, Alberta. He died in Vancouver on December 13, 1961, at the age of 67.

In 1939, Gray Campbell traded red serge for air-force blue, and piloted Lancaster bombers in 32 terrifying missions over Germany, earning medals he insisted his crew won for him. When the pilot climbed into his bomber, he held the briefcase of his former sergeant, Tommy Wallace, a gift from Tommy's widow. None of his frightful war experiences, Campbell admitted, "approached the nightmare I endured . . . when I stood silhouetted in the headlights, a clear target for the revolvers of three murderers." At war's end, Gray became a rancher in the Alberta foothills and wrote about it in *We Found Peace*. In the early 1960s, he established Gray's Publishing in Sidney, BC, producing 61 books over 20 years. He died in 2000.

Gray collected newspaper and pulp-magazine accounts of the 1935 case, pencilling in his own comments ("Nothing exciting ever happens in Banff in the fall"). Perhaps to make some sense of the anguished moments when "only the uniform held me together" as his "twenty-two year old world fell apart," he offered assistance to other writers. Twenty-five years later, former constable Jim Eaton suggested Gray write the story. "But what's the point?" Gray argued bitterly. "Tell the *whole* story," Eaton urged. So Gray Campbell tried. The result was a 2,500-word feature, "A Date With Murder." It was rejected by *Maclean's* magazine. But perhaps, by then, the rejection didn't matter; the piece had served its real purpose.

George "Nipper" Combe's police career took him to the northern outposts that Constable Gray Campbell had once dreamed about. While in Resolution and Reliance, Nipper never experienced anything remotely like the deadly events of 1935. In this, he was not unique. Nobody who endured the early 1930s would ever again experience the Depression's deprivation and violence, either in major cities or in little towns like Estevan, Benito or Blairmore, where, once upon a terrible time, fearful citizens watched Mounted Police, stetsons canted at rakish angles, clip-clop down Main Street.

Author's Note

Details of 1930s Banff, the turmoil caused by the zealot Sons of Freedom, various police actions and the killers' crimes can be found in a number of sources, although the details often conflict. The motivations and emotional states of people involved are more difficult—if not impossible—to confirm. I was often left with what I could prove or disprove and, given the era, circumstance and human nature, what I might deduce. What were the killers thinking? What went through Bill Neish's mind? Campbell's? The minds of senior RCMP officers? I asked myself: What was *most likely*? In formulating answers, I looked to their time and place, their personal backgrounds and situations.

One crime may still remain unsolved: did John Kalmakoff kill the Zurawells in 1933? This writer believes so, as did many others. The worst charges that Constable John Shaw could have laid against any of the three boys in Pelly that fateful night were minor ones for drunk driving or a firearms offence. A charge of robbery or attempted robbery would have been possible but unlikely. Two years later, authorities, newspapers and the public still believed none of these potential charges were serious enough to warrant the savage killings. Had Kalmakoff—alone, or with others—committed the Zurawell double murders?

The press and authorities admitted that much of the lives of the farm-boy killers were mysteries. Eighty years later, they remain so. The semi-literate boys recorded nothing. They wrote no "Dear Mom and Dad" letters as they tore across western Canada, outrunning the law. After conducting exhaustive interviews in four provinces, former Banff *Crag and Canyon* reporter Patricia Parker admitted, "I have been unable to discover what events triggered the [Shaw and Fawcett] murders."

However, neither she nor others mention the Zurawell murders or the fact that in November 1935 there was speculation that the RCMP planned to compare fingerprints found at the log house with those taken from the dead trio.

I discovered the possible link between Kalmakoff and the Zurawell murders in the *Yorkton Enterprise,* while researching (and disproving) "facts" of an earlier crime by Kalmakoff. Were the fingerprints from the Zurawell's house ever compared with those of the boys? If so, did they match? Does the crime remain unsolved to this day? Files held by the RCMP may answer these questions, but given today's stringent access-to-information regulations, prying those files open has been difficult and time-consuming. My attempts continue.

Readers looking for an account of the Banff shootout in RCMP retrospectives will be disappointed. The few accounts that exist are cursory. The RCMP's 1973 authorized book, *A Century of History,* which omits the Estevan, Saskatoon and Regina confrontations, also ignores this case. This seems odd considering its authors devote much space to Jack Cawsey and Dale, and when, for almost 70 years, it remained the deadliest case in RCMP history and inspired significant changes in the force's procedures. But given the troubling circumstances surrounding the tragic events, perhaps the omission is not surprising. I suspect it would be no surprise to warden Bill Neish.

Selected Bibliography

Books

Burton, Pierre. *The Great Depression 1929–1939*. Toronto: McClelland & Stewart, 1990.

Byfield, Ted, ed. *Alberta in the 20th Century*. Vol. 6, *Fury and Futility: The Onset of the Great Depression*. Edmonton: United Western Communications, 1998.

Gray, James H. *The Winter Years*. Toronto: MacMillan of Canada, 1966.

Hewitt, Steve. *Riding To the Rescue: The Transformation of the RCMP in Alberta and Saskatchewan 1914–1939*. Toronto: University of Toronto Press, 2006.

Howard, Victor. *We Were the Salt of the Earth*. Canadian Plains Research Center. Regina: University of Regina, 1985.

Parker, Patricia. *Dead Right, Dead Wrong*. Calgary: Benjamin Books, 1991.

Waiser, Bill. *All Hell Can't Stop Us: The On-to-Ottawa Trek and Regina Riot*. Calgary: Fifth House Ltd., 2003.

Newspapers

Calgary Herald
Calgary Albertan
Yorkton Enterprise

Unpublished Sources

Campbell, Gray. "Banff," "A Close Brush with Death," "A Date With Murder," "Writing A Wrong." Unpublished manuscripts. Gray Campbell Fonds. University of Victoria Libraries Special Collections.

Index

141

Acknowledgements

I extend gratitude to the authors who preserve Canada's Depression-era history, most recently, University of Saskatchewan history professor Bill Waiser, whose books reveal research of the highest order. Thanks to those at the Whyte Museum of the Rockies, Glenbow Archives, University of Victoria Special Collections, the archives of Alberta and Saskatchewan, the Calgary Public Library, and to those who read an early draft. Heartfelt thanks to the Campbell family, especially Gray's younger sister, Betty Eligh of Ottawa, who contributed valuable facts and insights. Most of all, appreciation to the late Gray A. Campbell, who saw it, felt it and wrote about it.

About the Author

Rich Mole is a former broadcaster, communications consultant and president of a Vancouver Island advertising agency. Fuelled by a lifelong fascination with history, he writes extensively about the events and people of Canada's past. Rich lives in Chilliwack, where he continues to write fiction. He welcomes readers' emailed comments at rich_mole@yahoo.com.

More Amazing Stories by Rich Mole

Scoundrels and Saloons: Whisky Wars of the Pacific Northwest, 1840–1917

print ISBN 978-1-927051-78-8
ebook ISBN 978-1-927051-79-5

Bootleggers, temperance crusaders and big business struggle for control of the liquor trade in frontier settlements of the Pacific Northwest.

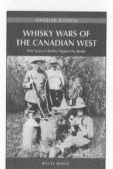

Whisky Wars of the Canadian West: Fifty Years of Battles Against the Bottle

print ISBN 978-1-926613-93-2
ebook ISBN 978-1-926936-99-4

From bootlegging to temperance movements, this is a fascinating account of a tumultuous era.

Visit heritagehouse.ca to see the entire list of books in this series.